ARK PAPERBACKS

C. G. JUNG

C. G. Jung (1875–1961), the Swiss psychiatrist and founder of Analytical Psychology, was an original thinker who made an immense contribution to the understanding of the human mind. In his early years he was a lecturer in psychiatry at the University of Zürich, and collaborated with Sigmund Freud. He gave up teaching to devote himself to his private practice in psychiatry and to research, eventually becoming world famous. He travelled widely and was a prolific author, often writing on subjects other than analytical psychology, such as mythology, alchemy, flying saucers, and the problem of time. Jung was also responsible for defining such influential and widely-used terms as the Collective Unconscious, Extraversion/Introversion, and Archetypes.

ARK

C. G. JUNG
THE PSYCHOLOGY OF THE OF THE TRANSFERENCE

TRANSLATED BY R.F.C. HULL

ARK PAPERBACKS

TO MY WIFE

First published in 1969 as The Psychology of the Transference
Extracted from Vol. 16 of the *Collected Works of C. G. Jung*
(second edition 1966)
ARK edition 1983
Reprinted 1989

ARK PAPERBACKS is an imprint of
Routledge
11 New Fetter Lane
London EC4P 4EE

Printed and bound in Great Britain by
Cox & Wyman Ltd, Reading

ISBN 0-7448-0006-4

EDITORIAL NOTE

C. G. Jung first published this work in book form as *Die Psychologie der Uebertragung* (Zurich: Rascher, 1946), and the present translation first appeared in Volume 16 of the *Collected Works* in 1954, together with eleven shorter papers on general and specific problems of psychotherapy. For the second edition, in 1966, the translation was extensively reworked and the footnotes and bibliography were corrected and brought up to date, taking into account the subsequent publication of nearly all of Jung's writings in the English edition.

In 1958 Volume 16, with the title *Praxis der Psychotherapie,* was the first volume to appear in the Swiss collected edition. In a foreword that Jung specially wrote for that volume he described *The Psychology of the Transference* as "an historical study of a phenomenon that may be regarded as the crux, or at any rate the crucial experience, in any thorough-going analysis—the problem of the transference, whose central importance was recognized long ago by Freud. This question is of such scope, and so difficult to elucidate in all its aspects, that a deeper investigation of its historical antecedents could not be avoided.

"Naturally, if an historical study like this is seen in isolation from my later writings, the unprepared reader will have some difficulty in recognizing its connection with his conception of what psychotherapy should be. Psychotherapeutic practice and the historical approach will seem to him to be two incommensurable things. In psychological reality, however, this is not the case at all, for we are constantly coming upon phenomena that reveal their historical character as soon as their causality is examined a little more closely. Psychic modes of behaviour are, indeed, of an eminently historical nature. The psychotherapist has to acquaint himself not only with the personal biography of his patient, but also with the mental and spiritual assumptions prevalent in his milieu, both present and past, where traditional and cultural influences play a part and often a decisive one.

"For example, no psychotherapist who seriously endeavours to understand the whole man is spared the task of learning the language of dreams and their symbolism. As with every language, historical knowledge is needed in order to understand it properly. This is particularly so since it is not an everyday language, but a symbolic language that makes frequent use of age-old forms of expression. A knowledge of these enables the analyst to extricate his patient from the oppressive constriction of a purely personalistic understanding of himself, and to release him from the egocentric prison that cuts him off from the wide horizon of his further social, moral, and spiritual development."

*

The paragraph numbers of the collected edition have been retained to facilitate reference, and some essential corrections have been made. The bibliography of Volume 16 is reproduced in full, inasmuch as only a few of its entries do not apply to *The Psychology of the Transference,* and a new index has been prepared.

TABLE OF CONTENTS

LIST OF ILLUSTRATIONS

Figures 1–10 are full pages, with woodcuts, reproduced from the *Rosarium philosophorum, secunda pars alchimiae de lapide philosophico* (Frankfurt, 1550). Figures 11–13 are full pages reproduced from the textless picture book *Mutus liber, in quo tamen tota philosophia hermetica . . . depingitur* (see Bibliography). They are described on page 160, note 1.

FOREWORD

veryone who has had practical experience of psychotherapy
nows that the process which Freud called "transference" often
resents a difficult problem. It is probably no exaggeration to
y that almost all cases requiring lengthy treatment gravitate
ound the phenomenon of transference, and that the success
r failure of the treatment appears to be bound up with it in
very fundamental way. Psychology, therefore, cannot very well
verlook or avoid this problem, nor should the psychotherapist
retend that the so-called "resolution of the transference" is
ust a matter of course. We meet with a similar optimism in the
reatment of "sublimation," a process closely connected with
he transference. In discussing these phenomena, people often
alk as though they could be dealt with by reason, or by intelli-
ence and will, or could be remedied by the ingenuity and art
f a doctor armed with superior technique. This euphemistic
nd propitiatory approach is useful enough when the situation
s not exactly simple and no easy results are to be had; but it
as the disadvantage of disguising the difficulty of the problem
nd thus preventing or postponing deeper investigation. Al-
hough I originally agreed with Freud that the importance of
he transference could hardly be overestimated, increasing ex-
erience has forced me to realize that its importance is relative.
he transference is like those medicines which are a panacea
or one and pure poison for another. In one case its appearance
enotes a change for the better, in another it is a hindrance and
n aggravation, if not a change for the worse, and in a third it
s relatively unimportant. Generally speaking, however, it is a
ritical phenomenon of varying shades of meaning and its ab-
ence is as significant as its presence.

In this book I am concerned with the "classical" form of
ransference and its phenomenology. As it is a form of relation-
hip, it always implies a vis-à-vis. Where it is negative or not
here at all, the vis-à-vis plays an unimportant part, as is gen-

erally the case, for instance, when there is an inferiority com plex coupled with a compensating need for self-assertion.[1]

It may seem strange to the reader that, in order to throw light on the transference, I should turn to something so ap parently remote as alchemical symbolism. But anyone who has read my book Psychology and Alchemy will know what close connections exist between alchemy and those phenomena which must, for practical reasons, be considered in the psychology of the unconscious. Consequently he will not be surprised to learn that this phenomenon, shown by experience to be so frequent and so important, also has its place in the symbolism and imagery of alchemy. Such images are not likely to be conscious representations of the transference relationship; rather, they unconsciously take that relationship for granted, and for this reason we may use them as an Ariadne thread to guide us in our argument.

The reader will not find an account of the clinical phenomena of transference in this book. It is not intended for the beginner who would first have to be instructed in such matters, but is addressed exclusively to those who have already gained sufficient experience from their own practice. My object is to provide some kind of orientation in this newly discovered and still unexplored territory, and to acquaint the reader with some of its problems. In view of the great difficulties that beset our understanding here, I would like to stress the provisional character of my investigation. I have tried to put together my observations and ideas, and I recommend them to the reader's consideration in the hope of directing his attention to certain points of view whose importance has forced itself upon me in the course of time. I am afraid that my description will not be easy reading for those who do not possess some knowledge of my earlier works. I have therefore indicated in the footnotes those of my writings which might be of assistance.

The reader who approaches this book more or less unpre-

---

[1] This is not to say that a transference never occurs in such cases. The negative form of transference in the guise of resistance, dislike, or hate endows the other person with great importance from the start, even if this importance is negative; and it tries to put every conceivable obstacle in the way of a positive transference. Consequently the symbolism so characteristic of the latter—the synthesis of opposites—cannot develop.

pared will perhaps be astonished at the amount of historical material I bring to bear on my investigation. The reason and inner necessity for this lie in the fact that it is only possible to come to a right understanding and appreciation of a contemporary psychological problem when we can reach a point outside our own time from which to observe it. This point can only be some past epoch that was concerned with the same problems, although under different conditions and in other forms. The comparative analysis thus made possible naturally demands a correspondingly detailed account of the historical aspects of the situation. These could be described much more succinctly if we were dealing with well-known material, where a few references and hints would suffice. But unfortunately that is not the case, since the psychology of alchemy here under review is almost virgin territory. I must therefore take it for granted that the reader has some knowledge of my Psychology and Alchemy, otherwise it will be hard for him to gain access to the present volume. The reader whose professional and personal experience has sufficiently acquainted him with the scope of the transference problem will forgive me this expectation.

Although the present study can stand on its own, it forms at the same time an introduction to a more comprehensive account of the problem of opposites in alchemy, and of their phenomenology and synthesis, which will appear later under the title Mysterium Coniunctionis.[2] I would like to express my thanks here to all those who read my manuscript and drew attention to defects. My particular thanks are due to Dr Marie-Louise von Franz for her generous help.

C. G. JUNG

Autumn, 1945

---

2 [Translated as Vol. 14 of the *Collected Works* (1963).]

THE PSYCHOLOGY OF THE TRANSFERENCE

INTERPRETED IN CONJUNCTION WITH
A SET OF ALCHEMICAL PICTURES

> *Quaero non pono, nihil hic determino dictans*
> *Coniicio, conor, confero, tento, rogo. . . .*
>
> (I inquire, I do not assert; I do not here
> determine anything with final assurance; I
> conjecture, try, compare, attempt, ask. . . .)
>
> —Motto to Christian Knorr von Rosenroth,
> *Adumbratio Kabbalae Christianae*

INTRODUCTION

Bellica pax, vulnus dulce, suave malum.
(A warring peace, a sweet wound, a mild evil.)
—JOHN GOWER, *Confessio amantis*, II, p. 35

1

The fact that the idea of the mystic marriage plays such an important part in alchemy is not so surprising when we remember that the term most frequently employed for it, *coniunctio,* referred in the first place to what we now call chemical combination, and that the substances or "bodies" to be combined were drawn together by what we would call affinity. In days gone by, people used a variety of terms which all expressed a human, and more particularly an erotic, relationship, such as *nuptiae, matrimonium, coniugium, amicitia, attractio, adulatio.* Accordingly the bodies to be combined were thought of as *agens et patiens,* as *vir* or *masculus,* and as *femina, mulier, femineus;* or they were described more picturesquely as dog and bitch,[1] horse (stallion) and donkey,[2] cock and hen,[3] and as the winged and wingless dragon.[4] The more anthropomorphic and theriomorphic the terms become, the more obvious is the part played by creative fantasy and thus by the unconscious, and

[1] "Accipe canem corascenum masculum et caniculum Armeniae" (Take a Corascene dog and an Armenian bitch).—"De alchimiae difficultatibus," *Theatrum chemicum,* I, p. 163. A quotation from Kalid (in the *Rosarium, Artis auriferae,* II, p. 248) runs: "Accipe canem coetaneum et catulam Armeniae" (Take a Coetanean dog and an Armenian bitch). In a magic papyrus, Selene (moon) is called κύων (bitch).—Paris MS. Z 2280, in Preisendanz, *Papyri Graecae Magicae,* I, p. 142. In Zosimos, dog and wolf.—Berthelot, *Alchimistes grecs,* III, xii, 9. [No translation of the words *corascenum* and *coetaneum* has been attempted, as we are advised that they are probably corrupt, or may indicate geographical names. —EDITORS.]

[2] Zosimos, in Berthelot, *Alch. grecs,* III, xii, 9.

[3] The classical passage is to be found in Senior, *De chemia,* p. 8: "Tu mei indiges, sicut gallus gallinae indiget" (You need me as the cock needs the hen).

[4] Numerous pictures exist in the literature.

3

the more we see how the natural philosophers of old were tempted, as their thoughts explored the dark, unknown qualities of matter, to slip away from a strictly chemical investigation and to fall under the spell of the "myth of matter." Since there can never be absolute freedom from prejudice, even the most objective and impartial investigator is liable to become the victim of some unconscious assumption upon entering a region where the darkness has never been illuminated and where he can recognize nothing. This need not necessarily be a misfortune, since the idea which then presents itself as a substitute for the unknown will take the form of an archaic though not inapposite analogy. Thus Kekulé's vision of the dancing couples,[5] which first put him on the track of the structure of certain carbon compounds, namely the benzene ring, was surely a vision of the *coniunctio,* the mating that had preoccupied the minds of the alchemists for seventeen centuries. It was precisely this image that had always lured the mind of the investigator away from the problem of chemistry and back to the ancient myth of the royal or divine marriage; but in Kekulé's vision it reached its chemical goal in the end, thus rendering the greatest imaginable service both to our understanding of organic compounds and to the subsequent unprecedented advances in synthetic chemistry. Looking back, we can say that the alchemists had keen noses when they made this *arcanum arcanorum,*[6] this *donum Dei et secretum altissimi,*[7] this inmost mystery of the art of gold-making, the climax of their work. The subsequent confirmation of the other idea central to gold-making—the transmutability of chemical elements—also takes a worthy place in this belated triumph of alchemical thought. Considering the eminently practical and theoretical importance of these two key ideas, we might well conclude that they were intuitive anticipations whose fascination can be explained in the light of later developments.[8]

---

[5] Kekulé, *Lehrbuch der organischen Chemie,* I, pp. 624f., and Fierz-David, *Die Entwicklungsgeschichte der Chemie,* pp. 235ff.

[6] Zacharius, "Opusculum," *Theatr. chem.,* I, p. 826.

[7] "Consilium coniugii," *Ars chemica,* p. 259. Cf. *Aurora consurgens,* I, Ch. II: "Est namque donum et sacramentum Dei atque res divina" (For she [Wisdom] is a gift and sacrament of God and a divine matter).

[8] This does not contradict the fact that the *coniunctio* motif owes its fascination primarily to its archetypal character.

We find, however, that alchemy did not merely change into chemistry by gradually discovering how to break away from its mythological premises, but that it also became, or had always been, a kind of mystic philosophy. The idea of the *coniunctio* served on the one hand to shed light on the mystery of chemical combination, while on the other it became the symbol of the *unio mystica,* since, as a mythologem, it expresses the archetype of the union of opposites. Now the archetypes do not represent anything external, non-psychic, although they do of course owe the concreteness of their imagery to impressions received from without. Rather, independently of, and sometimes in direct contrast to, the outward forms they may take, they represent the life and essence of a non-individual psyche. Although this psyche is innate in every individual it can neither be modified nor possessed by him personally. It is the same in the individual as it is in the crowd and ultimately in everybody. It is the precondition of each individual psyche, just as the sea is the carrier of the individual wave.

The alchemical image of the *coniunctio,* whose practical importance was proved at a later stage of development, is equally valuable from the psychological point of view: that is to say, it plays the same role in the exploration of the darkness of the psyche as it played in the investigation of the riddle of matter. Indeed, it could never have worked so effectively in the material world had it not already possessed the power to fascinate and thus to fix the attention of the investigator along those lines. The *coniunctio* is an *a priori* image that occupies a prominent place in the history of man's mental development. If we trace this idea back we find it has two sources in alchemy, one Christian, the other pagan. The Christian source is unmistakably the doctrine of Christ and the Church, *sponsus* and *sponsa,* where Christ takes the role of Sol and the Church that of Luna.[9] The pagan source is on the one hand the hierosgamos,[10] on the other the marital union of the mystic with God.[11] These psychic experiences and the traces they have left behind in tradition explain much that would otherwise

---

[9] Cf. the detailed account in Rahner, "Mysterium lunae."

[10] A collection of the classical sources is to be found in Klinz, Ἱερὸς γάμος.

[11] Bousset, *Hauptprobleme der Gnosis*, pp. 69ff., 263f., 315ff.; Leisegang, *Der heilige Geist*, I, p. 235.

be totally unintelligible in the strange world of alchemy and its secret language.

As we have said, the image of the *coniunctio* has always occupied an important place in the history of the human mind. Recent developments in medical psychology have, through observation of the mental processes in neuroses and psychoses, forced us to become more and more thorough in our investigation of the psychic background, commonly called the unconscious. It is psychotherapy above all that makes such investigations necessary, because it can no longer be denied that morbid disturbances of the psyche are not to be explained exclusively by the changes going on in the body or in the conscious mind; we must adduce a third factor by way of explanation, namely hypothetical unconscious processes.[12]

Practical analysis has shown that unconscious contents are invariably projected at first upon concrete persons and situations. Many projections can ultimately be integrated back into the individual once he has recognized their subjective origin; others resist integration, and although they may be detached from their original objects, they thereupon transfer themselves to the doctor. Among these contents the relation to the parent of opposite sex plays a particularly important part, i.e., the relation of son to mother, daughter to father, and also that of brother to sister.[13] As a rule this complex cannot be integrated completely, since the doctor is nearly always put in the place of the father, the brother, and even (though naturally more rarely) the mother. Experience has shown that this projection persists with all its original intensity (which Freud regarded as aetiological), thus creating a bond that corresponds in every respect to the initial infantile relationship, with a tendency to recapitulate all the experiences of childhood on the doctor. In other words, the neurotic maladjustment of the patient is now

12 I call unconscious processes "hypothetical" because the unconscious is by definition not amenable to direct observation and can only be inferred.

13 I am not considering the so-called homosexual forms, such as father-son, mother-daughter, etc. In alchemy, as far as I know, this variation is alluded to only once, in the "Visio Arislei" (*Art. aurif.*, I, p. 147): "Domine, quamvis rex sis, male tamen imperas et regis: masculos namque masculis coniunxisti, sciens quod masculi non gignunt" (Lord, though thou art king, yet thou rulest and governest badly; for thou hast joined males with males, knowing that males do not produce offspring).

transferred to him.[14] Freud, who was the first to recognize and describe this phenomenon, coined the term "transference neurosis."[15]

This bond is often of such intensity that we could almost speak of a "combination." When two chemical substances combine, both are altered. This is precisely what happens in the transference. Freud rightly recognized that this bond is of the greatest therapeutic importance in that it gives rise to a *mixtum compositum* of the doctor's own mental health and the patient's maladjustment. In Freudian technique the doctor tries to ward off the transference as much as possible—which is understandable enough from the human point of view, though in certain cases it may considerably impair the therapeutic effect. It is inevitable that the doctor should be influenced to a certain extent and even that his nervous health should suffer.[16]

---

[14] Freud says (*Introductory Lectures*, Part III, p. 455): "The decisive part of the work is achieved by creating in the patient's relation to the doctor—in the 'transference'—new editions of the old conflicts; in these the patient would like to behave in the same way as he did in the past. . . . In place of the patient's true illness there appears the artificially constructed transference illness, in place of the various unreal objects of his libido there appears a single, and once more imaginary, object in the person of the doctor." It is open to doubt whether the transference is always constructed artificially, since it is a phenomenon that can take place quite apart from any treatment, and is moreover a very frequent natural occurrence. Indeed, in any human relationship that is at all intimate, certain transference phenomena will almost always operate as helpful or disturbing factors.

[15] "Provided only that the patient shows compliance enough to respect the necessary conditions of the analysis, we regularly succeed in giving all the symptoms of the illness a new transference meaning and in replacing his ordinary neurosis by a 'transference-neurosis'. . . ." ("Remembering, Repeating, and Working-Through," p. 154.) Freud puts down a little too much to his own account here. A transference is not by any means always the work of the doctor. Often it is in full swing before he has even opened his mouth. Freud's conception of the transference as a "new edition of the old disorder," a "newly created and transformed neurosis," or a "new, artificial neurosis" (*Introductory Lectures*, III, p. 444), is right in so far as the transference of a neurotic patient is equally neurotic, but this neurosis is neither new nor artificial nor created: it is the same old neurosis, and the only new thing about it is that the doctor is now drawn into the vortex, more as its victim than as its creator.

[16] Freud had already discovered the phenomenon of the "counter-transference." Those acquainted with his technique will be aware of its marked tendency to keep the person of the doctor as far as possible beyond the reach of this effect.

He quite literally "takes over" the sufferings of his patient and shares them with him. For this reason he runs a risk—and must run it in the nature of things.[17] The enormous importance that Freud attached to the transference phenomenon became clear to me at our first personal meeting in 1907. After a conversation lasting many hours there came a pause. Suddenly he asked me out of the blue, "And what do you think about the transference?" I replied with the deepest conviction that it was the alpha and omega of the analytical method, whereupon he said, "Then you have grasped the main thing."

The great importance of the transference has often led to the mistaken idea that it is absolutely indispensable for a cure, that it must be demanded from the patient, so to speak. But a thing like that can no more be demanded than faith, which is only valuable when it is spontaneous. Enforced faith is nothing but spiritual cramp. Anyone who thinks that he must "demand" a transference is forgetting that this is only one of the therapeutic factors, and that the very word "transference" is closely akin to "projection"—a phenomenon that cannot possibly be demanded.[18] I personally am always glad when there is only a

---

Hence the doctor's preference for sitting behind the patient, also his pretence that the transference is a product of his technique, whereas in reality it is a perfectly natural phenomenon that can happen to him just as it can happen to the teacher, the clergyman, the general practitioner, and—last but not least—the husband. Freud also uses the expression "transference-neurosis" as a collective term for hysteria, hysterical fears, and compulsion neuroses (Ibid., p. 445).

17 The effects of this on the doctor or nurse can be very far-reaching. I know of cases where, in dealing with borderline schizophrenics, short psychotic intervals were actually "taken over," and during these periods it happened that the patients were feeling more than ordinarily well. I have even met a case of induced paranoia in a doctor who was analysing a woman patient in the early stages of latent persecution mania. This is not so astonishing since certain psychic disturbances can be extremely infectious if the doctor himself has a latent predisposition in that direction.

18 Freud himself says ("Observations on Transference-Love," p. 380) of this: "I can hardly imagine a more senseless proceeding. In doing so, an analyst robs the phenomenon of the element of spontaneity which is so convincing and lays up obstacles for himself in the future which are hard to overcome." Here Freud stresses the "spontaneity" of the transference, in contrast to his views quoted above. Nevertheless those who "demand" the transference can fall back on the following cryptic utterance of their master ("Fragment of an Analysis of a Case of Hysteria," p. 116): "If the theory of analytic technique is gone into, it becomes

8

mild transference or when it is practically unnoticeable. Far less claim is then made upon one as a person, and one can be satisfied with other therapeutically effective factors. Among these the patient's own insight plays an important part, also his goodwill, the doctor's authority, suggestion,[19] good advice,[20] understanding, sympathy, encouragement, etc. Naturally the more serious cases do not come into this category.

Careful analysis of the transference phenomenon yields an extremely complicated picture with such startlingly pronounced features that we are often tempted to pick out one of them as the most important and then exclaim by way of explanation: "Of course, it's nothing but . . . !" I am referring chiefly to the erotic or sexual aspect of transference fantasies. The existence of this aspect is undeniable, but it is not always the only one and not always the essential one. Another is the will to power (described by Adler), which proves to be coexistent with sexuality, and it is often very difficult to make out which of the two predominates. These two aspects alone offer sufficient grounds for a paralysing conflict.

There are, however, other forms of instinctive *concupiscentia* that come more from "hunger," from wanting to possess; others again are based on the instinctive negation of desire, so that life seems to be founded on fear or self-destruction. A certain *abaissement du niveau mental*, i.e., a weakness in the hierarchical order of the ego, is enough to set these instinctive urges and desires in motion and bring about a dissociation of personality—in other words, a multiplication of its centres of gravity. (In schizophrenia there is an actual fragmentation of personality.) These dynamic components must be regarded as real or symptomatic, vitally decisive or merely syndromal, according to the degree of their predominance. Although the strongest instincts undoubtedly demand concrete realization

---

evident that transference is [something necessarily demanded]." [". . . that transference is an inevitable necessity," as in the authorized translation, is to stretch the meaning of Freud's "etwas notwendig Gefordertes."—TRANS.]

[19] Suggestion happens of its own accord, without the doctor's being able to prevent it or taking the slightest trouble to produce it.

[20] "Good advice" is often a doubtful remedy, but generally not dangerous because it has so little effect. It is one of the things the public expects in the *persona medici*.

and generally enforce it, they cannot be considered exclusively biological since the course they actually follow is subject to powerful modifications coming from the personality itself. If a man's temperament inclines him to a spiritual attitude, even the concrete activity of the instincts will take on a certain symbolical character. This activity is no longer the mere satisfaction of instinctual impulses, for it is now associated with or complicated by "meanings." In the case of purely syndromal instinctive processes, which do not demand concrete realization to the same extent, the symbolical character of their fulfilment is all the more marked. The most vivid examples of these complications are probably to be found in erotic phenomenology. Four stages of eroticism were known in the late classical period: Hawwah (Eve), Helen (of Troy), the Virgin Mary, and Sophia. The series is repeated in Goethe's *Faust:* in the figures of Gretchen as the personification of a purely instinctual relationship (Eve); Helen as an anima figure; [21] Mary as the personification of the "heavenly," i.e., Christian or religious, relationship; and the "eternal feminine" as an expression of the alchemical *Sapientia.* As the nomenclature shows, we are dealing with the heterosexual Eros or anima-figure in four stages, and consequently with four stages of the Eros cult. The first stage—Hawwah, Eve, earth—is purely biological; woman is equated with the mother and only represents something to be fertilized. The second stage is still dominated by the sexual Eros, but on an aesthetic and romantic level where woman has already acquired some value as an individual. The third stage raises Eros to the heights of religious devotion and thus spiritualizes him: Hawwah has been replaced by spiritual motherhood. Finally, the fourth stage illustrates something which unexpectedly goes beyond the almost unsurpassable third stage: *Sapientia.* How can wisdom transcend the most holy and the most pure?—Presumably only by virtue of the truth that the less sometimes means the more. This stage represents a spiritualization of Helen and consequently of Eros as such. That is why *Sapientia* was regarded as a parallel to the Shulamite in the Song of Songs.

21 Simon Magus' Helen (Selene) is another excellent example.

2

Not only are there different instincts which cannot forcibly be reduced to one another, there are also different levels on which they move. In view of this far from simple situation, it is small wonder that the transference—also an instinctive process, in part—is very difficult to interpret and evaluate. The instincts and their specific fantasy-contents are partly concrete, partly symbolical (i.e., "unreal"), sometimes one, sometimes the other, and they have the same paradoxical character when they are projected. The transference is far from being a simple phenomenon with only one meaning, and we can never make out beforehand what it is all about. The same applies to its specific content, commonly called incest. We know that it is possible to interpret the fantasy-contents of the instincts either as *signs,* as self-portraits of the instincts, i.e., reductively; or as *symbols,* as the spiritual meaning of the natural instinct. In the former case the instinctive process is taken to be "real" and in the latter "unreal."

In any particular case it is often almost impossible to say what is "spirit" and what is "instinct." Together they form an impenetrable mass, a veritable magma sprung from the depths of primeval chaos. When one meets such contents one immediately understands why the psychic equilibrium of the neurotic is disturbed, and why the whole psychic system is broken up in schizophrenia. They emit a fascination which not only grips— and has already gripped—the patient, but can also have an inductive effect on the unconscious of the impartial spectator, in this case the doctor. The burden of these unconscious and chaotic contents lies heavy on the patient; for, although they are present in everybody, it is only in him that they have become active, and they isolate him in a spiritual loneliness which neither he nor anybody else can understand and which is bound to be misinterpreted. Unfortunately, if we do not feel our way into the situation and approach it purely from the outside, it is only too easy to dismiss it with a light word or to push it in the wrong direction. This is what the patient has long been doing on his own account, giving the doctor every opportunity for misinterpretation. At first the secret seems to lie with his

11

parents, but when this tie has been loosed and the projection withdrawn, the whole weight falls upon the doctor, who is faced with the question: "What are *you* going to do about the transference?"

The doctor, by voluntarily and consciously taking over the psychic sufferings of the patient, exposes himself to the overpowering contents of the unconscious and hence also to their inductive action. The case begins to "fascinate" him. Here again it is easy to explain this in terms of personal likes and dislikes, but one overlooks the fact that this would be an instance of *ignotum per ignotius*. In reality these personal feelings, if they exist at all in any decisive degree, are governed by those same unconscious contents which have become activated. An unconscious tie is established and now, in the patient's fantasies, it assumes all the forms and dimensions so profusely described in the literature. The patient, by bringing an activated unconscious content to bear upon the doctor, constellates the corresponding unconscious material in him, owing to the inductive effect which always emanates from projections in greater or lesser degree. Doctor and patient thus find themselves in a relationship founded on mutual unconsciousness.

It is none too easy for the doctor to make himself aware of this fact. One is naturally loath to admit that one could be affected in the most personal way by just any patient. But the more unconsciously this happens, the more the doctor will be tempted to adopt an "apotropaic" attitude, and the *persona medici* he hides behind is, or rather seems to be, an admirable instrument for this purpose. Inseparable from the *persona* is the doctor's routine and his trick of knowing everything beforehand, which is one of the favourite props of the well-versed practitioner and of all infallible authority. Yet this lack of insight is an ill counsellor, for the unconscious infection brings with it the therapeutic possibility—which should not be underestimated—of the illness being transferred to the doctor. We must suppose as a matter of course that the doctor is the better able to make the constellated contents conscious, otherwise it would only lead to mutual imprisonment in the same state of unconsciousness. The greatest difficulty here is that contents are often activated in the doctor which might normally remain latent. He might perhaps be so normal as not to need any such unconscious standpoints to compensate his conscious situation. At least this is often how it looks, though whether it is so in a deeper sense is an open question. Presumably he had good reasons for choosing the profession of psychiatrist and for being particularly interested in the treatment of the psychoneuroses; and he cannot very well do that without gaining some insight into his own unconscious processes. Nor can his concern with the unconscious be explained entirely by a free choice of interests, but rather by a fateful disposition which originally inclined him to the medical profession. The more one sees of human fate and the more one examines its secret springs of action, the more one is impressed by the strength of unconscious motives and by the limitations of free choice. The doctor knows—or at least he should know—that he did not choose this career by chance; and the psychotherapist in particular should clearly understand that psychic infections, however superfluous they seem to him, are in fact the predestined concomitants of his work, and thus fully in accord with the instinctive disposition of his own life. This realization also gives him the right attitude to his patient. The patient then means something to him personally, and this provides the most favourable basis for treatment.

3

In the old pre-analytical psychotherapy, going right back to the doctors of the Romantic Age, the transference was already defined as "rapport." It forms the basis of therapeutic influence once the patient's initial projections are dissolved. During this work it becomes clear that the projections can also obscure the judgment of the doctor—to a lesser extent, of course, for otherwise all therapy would be impossible. Although we may justifiably expect the doctor at the very least to be acquainted with the effects of the unconscious on his own person, and may therefore demand that anybody who intends to practise psychotherapy should first submit to a training analysis, yet even the best preparation will not suffice to teach him everything about the unconscious. A complete "emptying" of the unconscious is out of the question, if only because its creative powers are continually producing new formations.

Consciousness, no matter how extensive it may be, must always remain the smaller circle within the greater circle of the unconscious, an island surrounded by the sea; and, like the sea itself, the unconscious yields an endless and self-replenishing abundance of living creatures, a wealth beyond our fathoming. We may long have known the meaning, effects, and characteristics of unconscious contents without ever having fathomed their depths and potentialities, for they are capable of infinite variation and can never be depotentiated. The only way to get at them in practice is to try to attain a conscious attitude which allows the unconscious to co-operate instead of being driven into opposition.

Even the most experienced psychotherapist will discover again and again that he is caught up in a bond, a combination resting on mutual unconsciousness. And though he may believe himself to be in possession of all the necessary knowledge concerning the constellated archetypes, he will in the end come to realize that there are very many things indeed of which his academic knowledge never dreamed. Each new case that requires thorough treatment is pioneer work, and every trace of routine then proves to be a blind alley. Consequently the higher psychotherapy is a most exacting business and sometimes it sets tasks which challenge not only our understanding or our sympathy, but the whole man. The doctor is inclined to demand this total effort from his patient, yet he must realize that this same demand only works if he is aware that it applies also to himself.

I said earlier that the contents which enter into the transference were as a rule originally projected upon the parents or other members of the family. Owing to the fact that these contents seldom or never lack an erotic aspect or are genuinely sexual in substance (apart from the other factors already mentioned), an incestuous character does undoubtedly attach to them, and this has given rise to the Freudian theory of incest. Their exogamous transference to the doctor does not alter the situation. He is merely drawn into the peculiar atmosphere of family incest through the projection. This necessarily leads to an unreal intimacy which is highly distressing to both doctor and patient and arouses resistance and doubt on both sides. The violent repudiation of Freud's original discoveries gets

14

us nowhere, for we are dealing with an empirically demonstrable fact which meets with such universal confirmation that only the ignorant still try to oppose it. But the interpretation of this fact is, in the very nature of the case, highly controversial. Is it a genuine incestuous instinct or a pathological variation? Or is the incest one of the "arrangements" (Adler) of the will to power? Or is it regression of normal libido [22] to the infantile level, from fear of an apparently impossible task in life? [23] Or is all incest-fantasy purely symbolical, and thus a reactivation of the incest archetype, which plays such an important part in the history of the human mind?

For all these widely differing interpretations we can marshal more or less satisfactory arguments. The view which probably causes most offence is that incest is a genuine instinct. But, considering the almost universal prevalence of the incest taboo, we may legitimately remark that a thing which is not liked and desired generally requires no prohibition. In my opinion, each of these interpretations is justified up to a point, because all the corresponding shades of meaning are present in individual cases, though with varying intensity. Sometimes one aspect predominates and sometimes another. I am far from asserting that the above list could not be supplemented further.

In practice, however, it is of the utmost importance how the incestuous aspect is interpreted. The explanation will vary according to the nature of the case, the stage of treatment, the perspicacity of the patient, and the maturity of his judgment.

The existence of the incest element involves not only an intellectual difficulty but, worst of all, an emotional complication of the therapeutic situation. It is the hiding place for all the most secret, painful, intense, delicate, shamefaced, timorous, grotesque, unmoral, and at the same time the most sacred feelings which go to make up the indescribable and inexplicable wealth of human relationships and give them their compelling power. Like the tentacles of an octopus they twine themselves invisibly round parents and children and, through the trans-

---

[22] The reader will know that I do not understand *libido* in the original Freudian sense as *appetitus sexualis*, but as an *appetitus* which can be defined as psychic energy. See "On Psychic Energy."

[23] This is the view I have put forward as an explanation of certain processes in "The Theory of Psychoanalysis."

ference, round doctor and patient. This binding force shows itself in the irresistible strength and obstinacy of the neurotic symptom and in the patient's desperate clinging to the world of infancy or to the doctor. The word "possession" describes this state in a way that could hardly be bettered.

The remarkable effects produced by unconscious contents allow us to infer something about their energy. All unconscious contents, once they are activated—i.e., have made themselves felt—possess as it were a specific energy which enables them to manifest themselves everywhere (like the incest motif, for instance). But this energy is normally not sufficient to thrust the content into consciousness. For that there must be a certain predisposition on the part of the conscious mind, namely a deficit in the form of loss of energy. The energy so lost raises the psychic potency of certain compensating contents in the unconscious. The *abaissement du niveau mental,* the energy lost to consciousness, is a phenomenon which shows itself most drastically in the "loss of soul" among primitive peoples, who also have interesting psychotherapeutic methods for recapturing the soul that has gone astray. This is not the place to go into these matters in detail, so a bare mention must suffice.[24] Similar phenomena can be observed in civilized man. He too is liable to a sudden loss of initiative for no apparent reason. The discovery of the real reason is no easy task and generally leads to a somewhat ticklish discussion of things lying in the background. Carelessness of all kinds, neglected duties, tasks postponed, wilful outbursts of defiance, and so on, all these can dam up his vitality to such an extent that certain quanta of energy, no longer finding a conscious outlet, stream off into the unconscious, where they activate other, compensating contents, which in turn begin to exert a compulsive influence on the conscious mind. (Hence the very common combination of extreme neglect of duty and a compulsion neurosis.)

This is one way in which loss of energy may come about. The other way causes loss not through a malfunctioning of the conscious mind but through a "spontaneous" activation of unconscious contents, which react secondarily upon consciousness. There are moments in human life when a new page is turned.

[24] Cf. Frazer, *Taboo and the Perils of the Soul,* pp. 54ff.

New interests and tendencies appear which have hitherto received no attention, or there is a sudden change of personality (a so-called mutation of character). During the incubation period of such a change we can often observe a loss of conscious energy: the new development has drawn off the energy it needs from consciousness. This lowering of energy can be seen most clearly before the onset of certain psychoses and also in the empty stillness which precedes creative work.[25]

The remarkable potency of unconscious contents, therefore, always indicates a corresponding weakness in the conscious mind and its functions. It is as though the latter were threatened with impotence. For primitive man this danger is one of the most terrifying instances of "magic." So we can understand why this secret fear is also to be found among civilized people. In serious cases it is the secret fear of going mad; in less serious, the fear of the unconscious—a fear which even the normal person exhibits in his resistance to psychological views and explanations. This resistance borders on the grotesque when it comes to scouting all psychological explanations of art, philosophy, and religion, as though the human psyche had, or should have, absolutely nothing to do with these things. The doctor knows these well-defended zones from his consulting hours: they are reminiscent of island fortresses from which the neurotic tries to ward off the octopus. ("Happy neurosis island," as one of my patients called his conscious state!) The doctor is well aware that the patient needs an island and would be lost without it. It serves as a refuge for his consciousness and as the last stronghold against the threatening embrace of the unconscious. The same is true of the normal person's taboo regions which psychology must not touch. But since no war was ever won on the defensive, one must, in order to terminate hostilities, open negotiations with the enemy and see what his terms really are. Such is the intention of the doctor who volunteers to act as a mediator. He is far from wishing to disturb the somewhat precarious island idyll or pull down the fortifications. On the contrary, he is thankful that somewhere a firm foothold exists that does not first have to be fished up out of

[25] The same phenomenon can be seen on a smaller scale, but no less clearly, in the apprehension and depression which precede any special psychic exertion, such as an examination, a lecture, an important interview, etc.

the chaos, always a desperately difficult task. He knows that the island is a bit cramped and that life on it is pretty meagre and plagued with all sorts of imaginary wants because too much life has been left outside, and that as a result a terrifying monster is created, or rather is roused out of its slumbers. He also knows that this seemingly alarming animal stands in a secret compensatory relationship to the island and could supply everything that the island lacks.

The transference, however, alters the psychological stature of the doctor, though this is at first imperceptible to him. He too becomes affected, and has as much difficulty in distinguishing between the patient and what has taken possession of him as has the patient himself. This leads both of them to a direct confrontation with the daemonic forces lurking in the darkness. The resultant paradoxical blend of positive and negative, of trust and fear, of hope and doubt, of attraction and repulsion, is characteristic of the initial relationship. It is the νεῖκος καὶ φιλία (hate and love) of the elements, which the alchemists likened to the primeval chaos. The activated unconscious appears as a flurry of unleashed opposites and calls forth the attempt to reconcile them, so that, in the words of the alchemists, the great panacea, the *medicina catholica,* may be born.

4

It must be emphasized that in alchemy the dark initial state of *nigredo* is often regarded as the product of a previous operation, and that it therefore does not represent the absolute beginning.[26] Similarly, the psychological parallel to the *nigredo* is the result of the foregoing preliminary talk which, at a certain moment, sometimes long delayed, "touches" the uncon-

---

[26] Where the *nigredo* is identified with the *putrefactio* it does not come at the beginning, as for example in fig. 6 of our series of pictures from the *Rosarium philosophorum* (*Art. aurif.*, II, p. 254). In Mylius, *Philosophia reformata*, p. 116, the *nigredo* appears only in the fifth grade of the work, during the "putrefactio, quae in umbra purgatorii celebratur" (putrefaction which is celebrated in the darkness of Purgatory); but further on (p. 118), we read in contradiction to this: "Et haec denigratio est operis initium, putrefactionis indicium" etc. (And this *denigratio* is the beginning of the work, an indication of the putrefaction).

scious and establishes the unconscious identity [27] of doctor and patient. This moment *may* be perceived and registered consciously, but generally it happens outside consciousness and the bond thus established is recognized only later and indirectly by its results. Occasionally dreams occur about this time, announcing the appearance of the transference. For instance, a dream may say that a fire has started in the cellar, or that a burglar has broken in, or that the patient's father has died, or it may depict an erotic or some other ambiguous situation.[28] From the moment when such a dream occurs there may be initiated a queer unconscious time-reckoning, lasting for months or even longer. I have often observed this process and will give a practical instance of it:

When treating a lady of over sixty, I was struck by the following passage in a dream she had on October 21, 1938: "*A beautiful little child, a girl of six months old, is playing in the kitchen with her grandparents and myself, her mother. The grandparents are on the left of the room and the child stands on the square table in the middle of the kitchen. I stand by the table and play with the child. The old woman says she can hardly believe we have known the child for only six months. I say that it is not so strange because we knew and loved the child long before she was born.*"

It is immediately apparent that the child is something special, i.e., a child hero or divine child. The father is not mentioned; his absence is part of the picture.[29] The kitchen, as the scene of the happening, points to the unconscious. The square table is the quaternity, the classical basis of the "special" child,[30]

---

[27] "Unconscious identity" is the same as Lévy-Bruhl's *participation mystique*. Cf. *How Natives Think*.

[28] A pictorial representation of this moment, in the form of a flash of lightning and a "stone-birth," is to be found in my "A Study in the Process of Individuation," Picture 2.

[29] Because he is the "unknown father," a theme to be met with in Gnosticism. See Bousset, *Hauptprobleme der Gnosis*, Ch. II, pp. 58–91.

[30] Cf. Nicholas of Flüe's vision of the threefold fountain arising in the square container (Lavaud, *Vie profonde de Nicolas de Flue*, p. 67, and Stöckli, *Die Visionen des seligen Bruder Klaus*, p. 19). A Gnostic text says: "In the second Father[hood] the five trees are standing and in their midst is a trapeza [τράπεζα]. Standing on the trapeza is an Only-begotten word [λόγος μονογενής]." (Baynes, *A Coptic Gnostic Treatise*, p. 70.) The trapeza is an abbreviation of

for the child is a symbol of the self and the quaternity is a symbolical expression of this. The self as such is timeless and existed before any birth.[31] The dreamer was strongly influenced by Indian writings and knew the Upanishads well, but not the medieval Christian symbolism which is in question here. The precise age of the child made me ask the dreamer to look in her notes to see what had happened in the unconscious six months earlier. Under April 20, 1938, she found the following dream:

"With some other women I am looking at a piece of tapestry, a square with symbolical figures on it. Immediately afterwards I am sitting with some women in front of a marvellous tree. It is magnificently grown, at first it seems to be some kind of conifer, but then I think—in the dream—that it is a monkeypuzzle [a tree of genus *Araucaria*] *with the branches growing straight up like candles* [a confusion with *Cereus candelabrum*]. *A Christmas tree is fitted into it in such a way that at first it looks like one tree instead of two."*—As the dreamer was writing down this dream immediately on waking, with a vivid picture of the tree before her, she suddenly had a vision of a tiny golden child lying at the foot of the tree (tree-birth motif). She had thus gone on dreaming the sense of the dream. It undoubtedly depicts the birth of the divine ("golden") child.

But what had happened nine months previous to April 20, 1938? Between July 19 and 22, 1937, she had painted a picture showing, on the left, a heap of coloured and polished (precious) stones surmounted by a silver serpent, winged and crowned. In the middle of the picture there stands a naked female figure from whose genital region the same serpent rears up towards the heart, where it bursts into a five-pointed, gor-

---

τετράπεζα, a four-legged table or podium (ibid., p. 71). Cf. Irenaeus, *Contra haereses*, III, 11, where he compares the "fourfold gospel" with the four cherubim in the vision of Ezekiel, the four regions of the world, and the four winds: "ex quibus manifestum est, quoniam qui est omnium artifex Verbum, qui sedet super Cherubim et continet omnia, dedit nobis quadriforme Evangelium, quod uno spiritu continetur" (from which it is clear that He who is the Maker of all things, the Word [Logos] who sits above the Cherubim and holds all things together, gave unto us the fourfold gospel, which is contained in one spirit).

Concerning the kitchen, cf. Lavaud, *Vie profonde*, p. 66, and Stöckli, *Die Visionen*, p. 18.

[31] This is not a metaphysical statement but a psychological fact.

geously flashing golden star. A coloured bird flies down on the right with a little twig in its beak. On the twig five flowers are arranged in a *quaternio,* one yellow, one blue, one red, one green, but the topmost is golden—obviously a mandala structure.[32] The serpent represents the hissing ascent of Kundalini, and in the corresponding yoga this marks the first moment in a process which ends with deification in the divine Self, the syzygy of Shiva and Shakti.[33] It is obviously the moment of symbolical conception, which is both Tantric and—because of the bird—Christian in character, being a contamination of the symbolism of the Annunciation with Noah's dove and the sprig of olive.

This case, and more particularly the last image, is a classical example of the kind of symbolism which marks the onset of the transference. Noah's dove (the emblem of reconciliation), the *incarnatio Dei,* the union of God with matter for the purpose of begetting the redeemer, the serpent path, the Sushumna representing the line midway between sun and moon—all this is the first, anticipatory stage of an as-yet-unfulfilled programme that culminates in the union of opposites. This union is analogous to the "royal marriage" in alchemy. The prodromal events signify the meeting or collision of various opposites and can therefore appropriately be called chaos and blackness. As mentioned above, this may occur at the beginning of the treatment, or it may have to be preceded by a lengthy analysis, a stage of *rapprochement.* Such is particularly the case when the patient shows violent resistances coupled with fear of the activated contents of the unconscious.[34]

---

[32] As regards the bird with the flowering twig, see Figs. 2 and 3 infra.

[33] Avalon, *The Serpent Power,* pp. 345f.

[34] Freud, as we know, observes the transference problem from the standpoint of a personalistic psychology and thus overlooks the very essence of the transference —the collective contents of an archetypal nature. The reason for this is his notoriously negative attitude to the psychic reality of archetypal images, which he dismisses as "illusion." This materialistic bias precludes strict application of the phenomenological principle without which an objective study of the psyche is absolutely impossible. My handling of the transference problem, in contrast to Freud's, includes the archetypal aspect and thus gives rise to a totally different picture. Freud's rational treatment of the problem is quite logical as far as his purely personalistic premises go, but both in theory and in practice they do not go far enough, since they fail to do justice to the obvious admixture of archetypal data.

There is good reason and ample justification for these resistances and they should never, under any circumstances, be ridden over roughshod or otherwise argued out of existence. Neither should they be belittled, disparaged, or made ridiculous; on the contrary, they should be taken with the utmost seriousness as a vitally important defence mechanism against overpowering contents which are often very difficult to control. The general rule should be that the weakness of the conscious attitude is proportional to the strength of the resistance. When, therefore, there are strong resistances, the conscious rapport with the patient must be carefully watched, and—in certain cases—his conscious attitude must be supported to such a degree that, in view of later developments, one would be bound to charge oneself with the grossest inconsistency. That is inevitable, because one can never be too sure that the weak state of the patient's conscious mind will prove equal to the subsequent assault of the unconscious. In fact, one must go on supporting his conscious (or, as Freud thinks, "repressive") attitude until the patient can let the "repressed" contents rise up spontaneously. Should there by any chance be a latent psychosis [35] which cannot be detected beforehand, this cautious procedure may prevent the devastating invasion of the unconscious or at least catch it in time. At all events the doctor then has a clear conscience, knowing that he has done everything in his power to avoid a fatal outcome.[36] Nor is it beside the point to add that consistent support of the conscious attitude has in itself a high therapeutic value and not infrequently serves to bring about satisfactory results. It would be a dangerous prejudice to imagine that analysis of the unconscious is the one and only panacea which should therefore be employed in every case. It is rather like a surgical operation and we should only resort to the knife when other methods have failed. So long as it does not obtrude itself the unconscious is best left alone. The reader

[35] The numerical proportion of latent to manifest psychoses is about equal to that of latent to active cases of tuberculosis.
[36] The violent resistance, mentioned by Freud, to the rational resolution of the transference is often due to the fact that in some markedly sexual forms of transference there are concealed collective unconscious contents which defy all rational resolution. Or, if this resolution is successful, the patient is cut off from the collective unconscious and comes to feel this as a loss.

should be quite clear that my discussion of the transference problem is not an account of the daily routine of the psychotherapist, but far more a description of what happens when the check normally exerted on the unconscious by the conscious mind is disrupted, though this need not necessarily occur at all.

Cases where the archetypal problem of the transference becomes acute are by no means always "serious" cases, i.e., grave states of illness. There are of course such cases among them, but there are also mild neuroses, or simply psychological difficulties which we would be at a loss to diagnose. Curiously enough, it is these latter cases that present the doctor with the most difficult problems. Often the persons concerned endure unspeakable suffering without developing any neurotic symptoms that would entitle them to be called ill. We can only call it an intense suffering, a passion of the soul but not a disease of the mind.

5

Once an unconscious content is constellated, it tends to break down the relationship of conscious trust between doctor and patient by creating, through projection, an atmosphere of illusion which either leads to continual misinterpretations and misunderstandings, or else produces a most disconcerting impression of harmony. The latter is even more trying than the former, which at worst (though it is sometimes for the best!) can only hamper the treatment, whereas in the other case a tremendous effort is needed to discover the points of difference. But in either case the constellation of the unconscious is a troublesome factor. The situation is enveloped in a kind of fog, and this fully accords with the nature of the unconscious content: it is a "black blacker than black" (nigrum, nigrius nigro),[37] as the alchemists rightly say, and in addition is charged with dangerous polar tensions, with the *inimicitia elementorum*. One finds oneself in an impenetrable chaos, which is indeed one of the synonyms for the mysterious *prima materia*. The latter corresponds to the nature of the unconscious content in every respect, with one exception: this time it does not appear in the

---

[37] Cf. Lully, "Testamentum," *Bibliotheca chemica curiosa*, I, pp. 790ff., and Maier, *Symbola aureae mensae*, pp. 379f.

alchemical substance but in man himself. In the case of alchemy it is quite evident that the unconscious content is of human origin, as I have shown in *Psychology and Alchemy*.[38] Hunted for centuries and never found, the *prima materia* or *lapis philosophorum* is, as a few alchemists rightly suspected, to be discovered in man himself. But it seems that this content can never be found and integrated directly, but only by the circuitous route of projection. For as a rule the unconscious first appears in projected form. Whenever it appears to obtrude itself directly, as in visions, dreams, illuminations, psychoses, etc., these are always preceded by psychic conditions which give clear proof of projection. A classical example of this is Saul's fanatical persecution of the Christians before Christ appeared to him in a vision.

The elusive, deceptive, ever-changing content that possesses the patient like a demon now flits about from patient to doctor and, as the third party in the alliance, continues its game, sometimes impish and teasing, sometimes really diabolical. The alchemists aptly personified it as the wily god of revelation, Hermes or Mercurius; and though they lament over the way he hoodwinks them, they still give him the highest names, which bring him very near to deity.[39] But for all that, they deem themselves good Christians whose faithfulness of heart is never in doubt, and they begin and end their treatises with pious invocations.[40] Yet it would be an altogether unjustifiable suppression of the truth were I to confine myself to the negative

---

[38] Pars. 342f.

[39] Cf. "The Spirit Mercurius," Part II, sec. 6.

[40] Thus *Aurora consurgens*, II (*Art. aurif.*, I, pp. 185–246) closes with the words: "Et sic probata est medicina Philosophorum, quam omni [investiganti] fideli et pio praestare dignetur Deus omnipotens, unigenitusque filius Dei Dominus noster Jesus Christus, qui cum Patre et Spiritu sancto vivit et regnat, unus Deus per infinita saeculorum. Amen" (And this is the approved medicine of the philosophers, which may our Lord Jesus Christ, who liveth and reigneth with the Father and the Holy Ghost, one God for ever and ever, deign to give to every searcher who is faithful, pious, and of good will, Amen). This conclusion no doubt comes from the Offertorium (prayer during the *commixtio*), where it says: ". . . qui humanitatis nostrae fieri dignatus est particeps, Jesus Christus, Filius tuus, Dominus noster: qui tecum vivit et regnat in unitate Spiritus Sancti Deus per omnia saecula saeculorum. Amen." (. . . who vouchsafed to become partaker of our humanity, Jesus Christ, Thy Son, our Lord: who liveth and reigneth with Thee in the unity of the Holy Ghost, one God, world without end. Amen.)

description of Mercurius' impish drolleries, his inexhaustible invention, his insinuations, his intriguing ideas and schemes, his ambivalence and—often—his unmistakable malice. He is also capable of the exact opposite, and I can well understand why the alchemists endowed their Mercurius with the highest spiritual qualities, although these stand in flagrant contrast to his exceedingly shady character. The contents of the unconscious are indeed of the greatest importance, for the unconscious is after all the matrix of the human mind and its inventions. Wonderful and ingenious as this other side of the unconscious is, it can be most dangerously deceptive on account of its numinous nature. Involuntarily one thinks of the devils mentioned by St Athanasius in his life of St Anthony, who talk very piously, sing psalms, read the holy books, and—worst of all—speak the truth. The difficulties of our psychotherapeutic work teach us to take truth, goodness, and beauty where we find them. They are not always found where we look for them: often they are hidden in the dirt or are in the keeping of the dragon. "In stercore invenitur" (it is found in filth) [41] runs an alchemical dictum—nor is it any the less valuable on that account. But, it does not transfigure the dirt and does not diminish the evil, any more than these lessen God's gifts. The contrast is painful and the paradox bewildering. Sayings like

ουρανο ανω	(Heaven above
ουρανο κατω	Heaven below
αστρα ανω	Stars above
αστρα κατω	Stars below
παν ο ανω	All that is above
τουτο κατω	Also is below
ταυτα λαβε	Grasp this
κε ευτυχε	And rejoice) [42]

are too optimistic and superficial; they forget the moral torment occasioned by the opposites, and the importance of ethical values.

The refining of the *prima materia,* the unconscious con-

[41] Cf. "Tractatus aureus," *Ars chemica,* p. 21.
[42] Kircher, "Oedipus Aegyptiacus." II, Class X, Ch. V, p. 414. There is a connection between this text and the "Tabula smaragdina"; cf. Ruska, *Tabula smaragdina,* p. 217.

tent, demands endless patience, perseverance,[43] equanimity, knowledge, and ability on the part of the doctor; and, on the part of the patient, the putting forth of his best powers and a capacity for suffering which does not leave the doctor altogether unaffected. The deep meaning of the Christian virtues, especially the greatest among these, will become clear even to the unbeliever; for there are times when he needs them all if he is to rescue his consciousness, and his very life, from this pocket of chaos, whose final subjugation, without violence, is no ordinary task. If the work succeeds, it often works like a miracle, and one can understand what it was that prompted the alchemists to insert a heartfelt *Deo concedente* in their recipes, or to allow that only if God wrought a miracle could their procedure be brought to a successful conclusion.

6

It may seem strange to the reader that a "medical procedure" should give rise to such considerations. Although in illnesses of the body there is no remedy and no treatment that can be said to be infallible in all circumstances, there are still a great many which will probably have the desired effect without either doctor or patient having the slightest need to insert a *Deo concedente*. But we are not dealing here with the body —we are dealing with the psyche. Consequently we cannot speak the language of body-cells and bacteria; we need another language commensurate with the nature of the psyche, and equally we must have an attitude which measures the danger and can meet it. And all this must be genuine or it will have no effect; if it is hollow, it will damage both doctor and patient. The *Deo concedente* is not just a rhetorical flourish; it expresses the firm attitude of the man who does not imagine that he knows better on every occasion and who is fully aware that the un-

---

43 The *Rosarium* (*Art. aurif.*, II, p. 230) says: "Et scias, quod haec est longissima via, ergo patientia et mora sunt necessariae in nostro magisterio" (And you must know that this is a very long road; therefore patience and deliberation are needful in our magistery). Cf. *Aurora consurgens*, I, Ch. 10: "Tria sunt necessaria videlicet patientia mora et aptitudo instrumentorum" (Three things are necessary, namely: patience, deliberation, and skill with the instruments).

conscious material before him is something *alive*, a paradoxical Mercurius of whom an old master says: "Et est ille quem natura paululum operata est et in metallicam formam formavit, tamen imperfectum relinquit." (And he is that on whom nature hath worked but a little, and whom she hath wrought into metallic form yet left unfinished) [44]—a natural being, therefore, that longs for integration within the wholeness of a man. It is like a fragment of primeval psyche into which no consciousness has as yet penetrated to create division and order, a "united dual nature," as Goethe says—an abyss of ambiguities.

Since we cannot imagine—unless we have lost our critical faculties altogether—that mankind today has attained the highest possible degree of consciousness, there must be some potential unconscious psyche left over whose development would result in a further extension and a higher differentiation of consciousness. No one can say how great or small this "remnant" might be, for we have no means of measuring the possible range of conscious development, let alone the extent of the unconscious. But there is not the slightest doubt that a *massa confusa* of archaic and undifferentiated contents exists, which not only manifests itself in neuroses and psychoses but also forms the "skeleton in the cupboard" of innumerable people who are not really pathological. We are so accustomed to hear that everybody has his "difficulties and problems" that we simply accept it as a banal fact, without considering what these difficulties and problems really mean. Why is one never satisfied with oneself? Why is one unreasonable? Why is one not always good and why must one ever leave a cranny for evil? Why does one sometimes say too much and sometimes too little? Why does one do foolish things which could easily be avoided with a little forethought? What is it that is always frustrating us and thwarting our best intentions? Why are there people who never notice these things and cannot even admit their existence? And finally, why do people in the mass beget the historical lunacy of the last thirty years? Why couldn't Pythagoras, twenty-four hundred years ago, have established the rule of wisdom once and for all, or Christianity have set up the Kingdom of Heaven upon earth?

[44] *Rosarium*, p. 231. What the alchemist sees in "metallic form" the psychotherapist sees in man.

The Church has the doctrine of the devil, of an evil principle, whom we like to imagine complete with cloven hoofs, horns, and tail, half man, half beast, a chthonic deity apparently escaped from the rout of Dionysus, the sole surviving champion of the sinful joys of paganism. An excellent picture, and one which exactly describes the grotesque and sinister side of the unconscious; for we have never really come to grips with it and consequently it has remained in its original savage state. Probably no one today would still be rash enough to assert that the European is a lamblike creature and not possessed by a devil. The frightful records of our age are plain for all to see, and they surpass in hideousness everything that any previous age, with its feeble instruments, could have hoped to accomplish.

If, as many are fain to believe, the unconscious were only nefarious, only evil, then the situation would be simple and the path clear: to do good and to eschew evil. But what is "good" and what is "evil"? The unconscious is not just evil by nature, it is also the source of the highest good: [45] not only dark but also light, not only bestial, semi-human, and demonic but superhuman, spiritual, and, in the classical sense of the word, "divine." The Mercurius who personifies the unconscious [46] is essentially "duplex," paradoxically dualistic by nature, fiend, monster, beast, and at the same time panacea, "the philosophers' son," *sapientia Dei,* and *donum Spiritus Sancti.*[47]

Since this is so, all hope of a simple solution is abolished. All definitions of good and evil become suspect or actually invalid. As moral forces, good and evil remain unshaken, and —as the simple verities for which the penal code, the ten commandments, and conventional Christian morality take them— undoubted. But conflicting loyalties are much more subtle and

[45] Here I must expressly emphasize that I am not dabbling in metaphysics or discussing questions of faith, but am speaking of psychology. Whatever religious experience or metaphysical truth may be in themselves, looked at empirically they are essentially psychic phenomena, that is, they manifest themselves as such and must therefore be submitted to psychological criticism, evaluation, and investigation. Science comes to a stop at its *own* borders.

[46] Cf. "The Spirit Mercurius," Part II, sec. 10.

[47] The alchemists also liken him to Lucifer ("bringer of light"), God's fallen and most beautiful angel. Cf. Mylius, *Phil ref.,* p. 18.

dangerous things, and a conscience sharpened by worldly wisdom can no longer rest content with precepts, ideas, and fine words. When it has to deal with that remnant of primeval psyche, pregnant with the future and yearning for development, it grows uneasy and looks round for some guiding principle or fixed point. Indeed, once this stage has been reached in our dealings with the unconscious, these desiderata become a pressing necessity. Since the only salutary powers visible in the world today are the great psychotherapeutic systems which we call the religions, and from which we expect the soul's salvation, it is quite natural that many people should make the justifiable and often successful attempt to find a niche for themselves in one of the existing creeds and to acquire a deeper insight into the meaning of the traditional saving verities.

This solution is normal and satisfying in that the dogmatically formulated truths of the Christian Church express, almost perfectly, the nature of psychic experience. They are the repositories of the secrets of the soul, and this matchless knowledge is set forth in grand symbolical images. The unconscious thus possesses a natural affinity with the spiritual values of the Church, particularly in their dogmatic form, which owes its special character to centuries of theological controversy—absurd as this seemed in the eyes of later generations—and to the passionate efforts of many great men.

7

The Church would be an ideal solution for anyone seeking a suitable receptacle for the chaos of the unconscious were it not that everything man-made, however refined, has its imperfections. The fact is that a return to the Church, i.e., to a particular creed, is not the general rule. Much the more frequent is a better understanding of, and a more intense relation to, religion as such, which is not to be confused with a creed.[48] This, it seems to me, is mainly because anyone who appreciates the legitimacy of the two viewpoints, of the two branches into which Christianity has been split, cannot maintain the exclu-

[48] Cf. "Psychology and Religion," pars. 6f.

sive validity of either of them, for to do so would be to deceive himself. As a Christian, he has to recognize that the Christendom he belongs to has been split for four hundred years and that his Christian beliefs, far from redeeming him, have exposed him to a conflict and a division that are still rending the body of Christ. These are the facts, and they cannot be abolished by each creed pressing for a decision in its favour, as though each were perfectly sure it possessed the absolute truth. Such an attitude is unfair to modern man; he can see very well the advantages that Protestantism has over Catholicism and *vice versa*, and it is painfully clear to him that this sectarian insistence is trying to corner him against his better judgment—in other words, tempting him to sin against the Holy Ghost. He even understands why the churches are bound to behave in this way, and knows that it must be so lest any joyful Christian should imagine himself already reposing in Abraham's anticipated bosom, saved and at peace and free from all fear. Christ's passion continues—for the life of Christ in the *corpus mysticum,* or Christian life in both camps, is at loggerheads with itself and no honest man can deny the split. We are thus in the precise situation of the neurotic who must put up with the painful realization that he is in the midst of conflict. His repeated efforts to repress the other side have only made his neurosis worse. The doctor must advise him to accept the conflict just as it is, with all the suffering this inevitably entails, otherwise the conflict will never be ended. Intelligent Europeans, if at all interested in such questions, are consciously or semiconsciously protestant Catholics and catholic Protestants, nor are they any the worse for that. It is no use telling me that no such people exist: I have seen both sorts, and they have considerably raised my hopes about the European of the future.

But the negative attitude of the public at large to all credos seems to be less the result of religious convictions than one symptom of the general mental sloth and ignorance of religion. We can wax indignant over man's notorious lack of spirituality, but when one is a doctor one does not invariably think that the disease is malevolent or the patient morally inferior; instead, one supposes that the negative results may possibly be due to the remedy applied. Although it may reasonably be doubted whether man has made any marked or even perceptible progress in morality during the known five thousand years of human civilization, it cannot be denied that there has been a notable development of consciousness and its functions. Above all, there has been a tremendous extension of consciousness in the form of *knowledge*. Not only have the individual functions become differentiated, but to a large extent they have been brought under the control of the ego—in other words, man's will has developed. This is particularly striking when we compare our mentality with that of primitives. The security of our ego has, in comparison with earlier times, greatly increased and has even taken such a dangerous leap forward that, although we sometimes speak of "God's will," we no longer know what we are saying, for in the same breath we assert, "Where there's a will there's a way." And who would ever think of appealing to God's help rather than to the goodwill, the sense of responsibility and duty, the reason or intelligence, of his fellow men?

Whatever we may think of these changes of outlook, we cannot alter the fact of their existence. Now when there is a marked change in the individual's state of consciousness, the unconscious contents which are thereby constellated will also change. And the further the conscious situation moves away from a certain point of equilibrium, the more forceful and accordingly the more dangerous become the unconscious contents that are struggling to restore the balance. This leads ultimately to a dissociation: on the one hand, ego-consciousness makes convulsive efforts to shake off an invisible opponent (if it does not suspect its next-door neighbour of being the devil!), while on the other hand it increasingly falls victim to the tyrannical will of an internal "Government opposition" which displays all the characteristics of a dæmonic subman and superman combined.

When a few million people get into this state, it produces the sort of situation which has afforded us such an edifying object-lesson every day for the last ten years. These contemporary events betray their psychological background by their very singularity. The insensate destruction and devastation are a reaction against the deflection of consciousness from the point of equilibrium. For an equilibrium does in fact exist between the psychic ego and non-ego, and that equilibrium is a *religio*, a "careful consideration" [49] of ever-present unconscious forces which we neglect at our peril. The present crisis has been brewing for centuries because of this shift in man's conscious situation.

Have the Churches adapted themselves to this secular change? Their truth may, with more right than we realize, call itself "eternal," but its temporal garment must pay tribute to the evanescence of all earthly things and should take account of psychic changes. Eternal truth needs a human language that alters with the spirit of the times. The primordial images undergo ceaseless transformation and yet remain ever the same, but only in a new form can they be understood anew. Always they require a new interpretation if, as each formulation becomes obsolete, they are not to lose their spellbinding power over that *fugax Mercurius* [50] and allow that useful though dangerous enemy to escape. What is that about "new wine in old bottles"? Where are the answers to the spiritual needs and troubles of a new epoch? And where the knowledge to deal with the psychological problems raised by the development of modern consciousness? Never before has eternal truth been faced with such a hybris of will and power.

8

Here, apart from motives of a more personal nature, probably lie the deeper reasons for the fact that the greater part of Europe has succumbed to neo-paganism and anti-Christianity, and has set up a religious ideal of worldly power in opposition to the metaphysical ideal founded on love. But the individual's decision not to belong to a Church does not necessarily denote an anti-Christian attitude; it may mean exactly the reverse: a reconsidering of the kingdom of God in the human heart where, in the words of St. Augustine,[51] the *mysterium paschale* is accomplished "in its inward and higher meanings." The ancient and long obsolete idea of man as a microcosm contains a supreme psychological truth that has yet to be discov-

49 I use the classical etymology of *religio* and not that of the Church Fathers.
50 Maier, *Symb. aur. mens.*, p. 386.
51 *Epistula LV* (Migne, *P.L.*, vol. 33, cols. 208–09).

ered. In former times this truth was projected upon the body, just as alchemy projected the unconscious psyche upon chemical substances. But it is altogether different when the microcosm is understood as that interior world whose inward nature is fleetingly glimpsed in the unconscious. An inkling of this is to be found in the words of Origen: "Intellige te alium mundum esse in parvo et esse intra te Solem, esse Lunam, esse etiam stellas" (Understand that thou art a second little world and that the sun and the moon are within thee, and also the stars).[52] And just as the cosmos is not a dissolving mass of particles, but rests in the unity of God's embrace, so man must not dissolve into a whirl of warring possibilities and tendencies imposed on him by the unconscious, but must become the unity that embraces them all. Origen says pertinently: "Vides, quomodo ille, qui putatur unus esse, non est unus, sed tot in eo personae videntur esse, quot mores" (Thou seest that he who seemeth to be one is yet not one, but as many persons appear in him as he hath velleities).[53] Possession by the unconscious means being torn apart into many people and things, a *disiunctio*. That is why, according to Origen, the aim of the Christian is to become an inwardly united human being.[54] The blind insistence on the outward community of the Church naturally fails to fulfil this aim; on the contrary, it inadvertently provides the inner disunity with an outward vessel without really changing the *disiunctio* into a *coniunctio*.

The painful conflict that begins with the *nigredo* or *tenebrositas* is described by the alchemists as the *separatio* or *divisio elementorum*, the *solutio, calcinatio, incineratio,* or as dismemberment of the body, excruciating animal sacrifices, amputation of the mother's hands or the lion's paws, atomization of the bridegroom in the body of the bride, and so on.[55] While this extreme form of *disiunctio* is going on, there is a transformation of that arcanum—be it substance or spirit—which invariably turns out to be the mysterious Mercurius. In other words, out of the monstrous animal forms there gradually emerges a *res simplex*, whose nature is one and the same and yet consists

[52] *Homiliae in Leviticum*, V, 2 (Migne, *P.G.*, vol. 12, col. 449).
[53] Ibid.
[54] *Hom. in Librum Regnorum*, 1, 4.
[55] "Hounded from one bride-chamber to the next."—*Faust*, Part I.

of a duality (Goethe's "united dual nature"). The alchemist tries to get round this paradox or antinomy with his various procedures and formulae, and to make one out of two.[56] But the very multiplicity of his symbols and symbolic processes proves that success is doubtful. Seldom do we find symbols of the goal whose dual nature is not immediately apparent. His *filius philosophorum,* his *lapis,* his *rebis,* his homunculus, are all hermaphroditic. His gold is *non vulgi,* his *lapis* is spirit and body, and so is his tincture, which is a *sanguis spiritualis*—a spiritual blood.[57] We can therefore understand why the *nuptiae chymicae,* the royal marriage, occupies such an important place in alchemy as a symbol of the supreme and ultimate union, since it represents the magic-by-analogy which is supposed to bring the work to its final consummation and bind the opposites by love, for "love is stronger than death."

9

Alchemy describes, not merely in general outline but often in the most astonishing detail, the same psychological phenomenology which can be observed in the analysis of unconscious processes. The individual's specious unity that emphatically says "*I* want, *I* think" breaks down under the impact of the unconscious. So long as the patient can think that somebody else (his father or mother) is responsible for his difficulties, he can save some semblance of unity (*putatur unus esse!*). But once he realizes that he himself has a shadow, that his enemy is in his own heart, then the conflict begins and one becomes two. Since the "other" will eventually prove to be yet another duality, a compound of opposites, the ego soon becomes a shuttlecock tossed between a multitude of "velleities," with the result that there is an "obfuscation of the light," i.e., consciousness is depotentiated and the patient is at a loss to know where his personality begins or ends. It is like passing through the valley of the shadow, and sometimes the patient has to cling to

[56] For the same process in the individual psyche, see *Psychology and Alchemy,* pars. 44ff.
[57] Cf. Ruska, *Turba,* Sermo XIX, p. 129. The term comes from the Book of El-Habib (ibid., p. 43).

the doctor as the last remaining shred of reality. This situation is difficult and distressing for both parties; often the doctor is in much the same position as the alchemist who no longer knew whether he was melting the mysterious amalgam in the crucible or whether he was the salamander glowing in the fire. Psychological induction inevitably causes the two parties to get involved in the transformation of the third and to be themselves transformed in the process, and all the time the doctor's knowledge, like a flickering lamp, is the one dim light in the darkness. Nothing gives a better picture of the psychological state of the alchemist than the division of his work-room into a "laboratory," where he bustles about with crucibles and alembics, and an "oratory," where he prays to God for the much needed illumination—"purge the horrible darknesses of our mind," [58] as the author of *Aurora* quotes.

"Ars requirit totum hominem," we read in an old treatise.[59] This is in the highest degree true of psychotherapeutic work. A genuine participation, going right beyond professional routine, is absolutely imperative, unless of course the doctor prefers to jeopardize the whole proceeding by evading his own problems, which are becoming more and more insistent. The doctor must go to the limits of his subjective possibilities, otherwise the patient will be unable to follow suit. Arbitrary limits are no use, only real ones. It must be a genuine process of purification where "all superfluities are consumed in the fire" and the basic facts emerge. Is there anything more fundamental than the realization, "This is what I am"? It reveals a unity which nevertheless is—or was—a diversity. No longer the earlier ego with its make-believes and artificial contrivances, but another, "objective" ego, which for this reason is better called the "self." No longer a mere selection of suitable fictions, but a string of hard facts, which together make up the cross we all have to carry or the fate we ourselves are. These first indications of a future synthesis of personality, as I have shown in my earlier publications, appear in dreams or in "active imagination," where they

---

[58] "Spiritus alme,/illustrator hominum,/horridas nostrae/mentis purga tenebras." (Sublime spirit, enlightener of mankind, purge the horrible darknesses of our mind.)—Notker Balbulus, *Hymnus in Die Pentecostes* (Migne, *P.L.*, vol. 131, cols. 1012–13).

[59] Hoghelande, "De alchemiae difficultatibus," p. 139.

take the form of the mandala symbols which were also not unknown in alchemy. But the first signs of this symbolism are far
from indicating that unity has been attained. Just as alchemy
has a great many very different procedures, ranging from the
sevenfold to the thousandfold distillation, or from the "work
of one day" to "the errant quest" lasting for decades, so the
tensions between the psychic pairs of opposites ease off only
gradually; and, like the alchemical end-product, which always
betrays its essential duality, the united personality will never
quite lose the painful sense of innate discord. Complete redemption from the sufferings of this world is and must remain
an illusion. Christ's earthly life likewise ended, not in compla-
cent bliss, but on the cross. (It is a remarkable fact that in their
hedonistic aims materialism and a certain species of "joyful"
Christianity join hands like brothers.) The goal is important
only as an idea; the essential thing is the *opus* which leads to the
goal: *that* is the goal of a lifetime. In its attainment "left and
right" [60] are united, and conscious and unconscious work in
harmony.

10

The *coniunctio oppositorum* in the guise of Sol and Luna,
the royal brother-sister or mother-son pair, occupies such an
important place in alchemy that sometimes the entire process
takes the form of the *hierosgamos* and its mystic consequences.
The most complete and the simplest illustration of this is perhaps the series of pictures contained in the *Rosarium philosophorum* of 1550, which series I reproduce in what follows.
Its psychological importance justifies closer examination. Everything that the doctor discovers and experiences when analysing
the unconscious of his patient coincides in the most remarkable
way with the content of these pictures. This is not likely to be
mere chance, because the old alchemists were often doctors as

---

[60] *Acta Joannis*, 98 (cf. James, *Apocryphal New Testament*, p. 255): . . . καὶ
ἁρμονία σοφίας· σοφία δὲ οὖσα ἐν ἁρμονίᾳ ὑπάρχουσιν δεξιοὶ καὶ ἀριστεροί, δυνάμεις,
ἐξουσίαι, ἀρχαὶ καὶ δαίμονες, ἐνέργειαι . . . (". . . Harmony of wisdom, but when
there is wisdom the left and the right are in harmony: powers, principalities,
archons, daemons, forces . . .").

well, and thus had ample opportunity for such experiences if, like Paracelsus, they worried about the psychological well-being of their patients or inquired into their dreams (for the purpose of diagnosis, prognosis, and therapy). In this way they could collect information of a psychological nature, not only from their patients but also from themselves, i.e., from the observation of their own unconscious contents which had been activated by induction.[61] Just as the unconscious expresses itself even today in a picture-series, often drawn spontaneously by the patient, so those earlier pictures, such as we find in the Codex Rhenoviensis 172, in Zurich, and in other treatises, were no doubt produced in a similar way, that is, as the deposit of impressions collected during the work and then interpreted or modified in the light of traditional factors.[62] In the modern pictures, too, we find not a few traces of traditional themes side by side with spontaneous repetitions of archaic or mythological ideas. In view of this close connection between picture and psychic content, it does not seem to me out of place to examine a medieval series of pictures in the light of modern discoveries, or even to use them as an Ariadne thread in our account of the latter. These curiosities of the Middle Ages contain the seeds of much that emerged in clearer form only many centuries later.

[61] Cardan (*Somniorum synesiorum . . .*) is an excellent example of one who examined his own dreams.

[62] As regards the work of reinterpretation, see my "Brother Klaus." Also Lavaud, *Vie profonde*, Ch. III, "La Grande Vision."

AN ACCOUNT OF THE TRANSFERENCE PHENOMENA BASED ON THE ILLUSTRATIONS TO THE "ROSARIUM PHILOSOPHORUM"

> *Invenit gratiam in deserto populus. . . .*
> —JEREMIAS (VULGATE) 31 : 2
> The people . . . found grace in the desert. . . .
> —JEREMIAS (D.V.) 31 : 2

1

THE MERCURIAL FOUNTAIN

We are the metals' first nature and only source/
The highest tincture of the Art is made through us.
No fountain and no water has my like/
I make both rich and poor both whole and sick.
For healthful can I be and poisonous.[1]

[*Figure 1*]

This picture goes straight to the heart of alchemical symbolism, for it is an attempt to depict the mysterious basis of the
opus. It is a quadratic quaternity characterized by the four
stars in the four corners. These are the four elements. Above,
in the centre, there is a fifth star which represents the fifth
entity, the "One" derived from the four, the *quinta essentia*.
The basin below is the *vas Hermeticum*, where the transformation takes place. It contains the *mare nostrum*, the *aqua permanens* or ὕδωρ θεῖον, the "divine water." This is the *mare tene-
brosum*, the chaos. The vessel is also called the uterus[2] in

[1] [These mottoes, where they appear, translate the verses under the woodcuts in
the figures. Figs. 1–10 are full pages reproduced from the Frankfurt first edition
(1550) of the *Rosarium philosophorum*. The textual quotations, however, are
taken from the version printed in *Art. aurif.*, II (Basel, 1593), except for the poem
at par. 528.—EDITORS.]

[2] The "Cons. coniug." (*Ars chemica*, p. 147) says: "Et locus generationis, licet sit
artificialis, tamen imitatur naturalem, quia est concavus, conclusus" etc. (The
place of gestation, even though it is artificial, yet imitates the natural place, since
it is concave and closed). And (p. 204): "Per matricem, intendit fundum
cucurbitae" (By matrix he means the root of the gourd).

which the *foetus spagyricus* (the homunculus) is gestated.[3] This basin, in contrast to the surrounding square, is circular, because it is the matrix of the perfect form into which the square, as an imperfect form, must be changed. In the square the elements are still separate and hostile to one another and must therefore be united in the circle. The inscription on the rim of the basin bears out this intention. It runs (filling in the abbreviations): "Unus est Mercurius mineralis, Mercurius vegetabilis, Mercurius animalis." (*Vegetabilis* should be translated as "living" and *animalis* as "animate" in the sense of having a soul, or even as "psychic." [4]) On the outside of the basin there are six stars which together with Mercurius represent the seven planets or metals. They are all as it were contained in Mercurius, since he is the *pater metallorum*. When personified, he is the unity of the seven planets, an Anthropos whose body is the world, like Gayomart, from whose body the seven metals flow into the earth. Owing to his feminine nature, Mercurius is also the mother of the seven, and not only of the six, for he is his own father and mother.[5]

Out of the "sea," then, there rises this Mercurial Fountain, *triplex nomine,* as is said with reference to the three manifestations of Mercurius.[6] He is shown flowing out of three

---

[3] Cf. Ruska, *Turba,* p. 163.

[4] Cf. Hortulanus (Ruska, *Tabula smaragdina,* p. 186): "Unde infinitae sunt partes mundi, quas omnes philosophus in tres partes dividit scil. in partem Mineralem Vegetabilem et Animalem. . . . Et ideo dicit habens tres partes philosophiae totius mundi, quae partes continentur in unico lapide scil. Mercurio Philosophorum" (Hence the parts of the world are infinite, all of which the philosopher divides into three parts, namely mineral, vegetable, animal. . . . And therefore he claims to have the three parts of the philosophy of the whole world, which parts are contained in the single stone, namely the Mercurius of the Philosophers). Ch. 13: "Et ideo vocatur lapis iste perfectus, quia in se habet naturam mineralium et vegetabilium et animalium. Est enim lapis triunus et unus, quatuor habens naturas" (And this stone is called perfect because it has in itself the nature of mineral, vegetable, and animal. For the stone is triple and one, having four natures).

[5] Cf. the alchemical doctrine of the *increatum: Psychology and Alchemy,* pars. 430ff.

[6] A quotation based on Rosinus in *Rosarium,* p. 249, says: "Triplex in nomine, unus in esse." Cf. the threefold fountain of God in the vision of Brother Klaus (Lavaud, *Vie profonde,* p. 66). The actual Rosinus passage (itself a quotation from Rhazes) runs (*Art. aurif.,* I, p. 300): "Lapis noster cum mundi creato[re]

ROSARIVM

Wyr sindt der metall anfang vnd erste natur/
Die kunst macht durch vns die höchste tinctur.
Keyn brunn noch wasser ist meyn gleych/
Ich mach gesund arm vnd reych.
Vnd bin doch jtzund gyftig vnd dötlich.

Succus

Figure 1

pipes in the form of *lac virginis, acetum fontis,* and *aqua vitae.*
These are three of his innumerable synonyms. The aforementioned unity of Mercurius is here represented as a triad. It is
repeatedly emphasized that he is a trinity, *triunus* or *trinus,* the
chthonic, lower, or even infernal counterpart of the Heavenly
Trinity, just as Dante's devil is three-headed.[7] For the same
reason Mercurius is often shown as a three-headed serpent.
Above the three pipes we find the sun and moon, who are the
indispensable acolytes and parents of the mystic transformation, and, a little higher, the quintessential star, symbol of the
unity of the four hostile elements. At the top of the picture is
the *serpens bifidus,* the divided (or two-headed) serpent, the
fatal *binarius* which Dorn defines as the devil.[8] This serpent is
the *serpens mercurialis,*[9] representing the *duplex natura* of
Mercurius. The heads are spitting forth fire, from which Maria
the Copt or Jewess derived her "duo fumi." [10] These are the two
vapours whose condensation [11] initiates the process which leads
to a multiple sublimation or distillation for the purpose of

---

nomen habet, qui est trinus et unus" (Our stone has a name common with the
Creator of the world who is triple and one). Senior (*De chemia,* p. 45) says:
"Aes nostrum est sicut homo, habens spiritum, animam et corpus. Propterea
dicunt sapientes: Tria et Tria sunt unum. Deinde dixerunt: in uno sunt tria."
(Our copper is like a man, having spirit, soul, and body. Therefore the wise men
say: Three and Three are One. Further they said: In One there are Three.) Cf.
also Zosimos (Berthelot, *Alch. grecs,* III, vi, 18). The mercurial fountain recalls
the πηγὴ μεγάλη of the Peratics (Hippolytus, *Elenchos,* V, 12, 2), which forms
one part of the threefold world. The three parts correspond to 3 gods, 3 λόγοι,
3 spirits (νοῖ), 3 men. This triad is opposed by a Christ equipped with all the
properties of the triad and himself of triadic nature, coming from above, from
the ἀγεννησία, before the separation. (Here I prefer Bernays' reading πρὸ τῆς [cf.
Elenchos, p. 105] because it makes more sense.)

7 In Abū'l-Qāsim the lapis is called *al-shaitan,* 'Satan'; cf. Holmyard, "Abū'l-
Qāsim al-Irāqī," p. 422.

8 The serpent is also *triplex nomine,* as the inscriptions "animalis," "vegetabilis,"
"mineralis" show.

9 *Psychology and Alchemy,* fig. 20.

10 "Practica," *Art. aurif.,* I, p. 321: "Ipsa sunt duo fumi complectentes duo
lumina" (They are the two vapours enveloping the two lights).

11 We find the same motif in the title-page of Colonna, *Le Songe de Poliphile,*
as the leaves which fall from the tree rooted in the fire. See *Psychology and
Alchemy,* fig. 4.

purifying away the *mali odores*, the *foetor sepulcrorum*,[12] and the clinging darkness of the beginning.

This structure reveals the *tetrameria* (fourfold nature) of the transforming process, already known to the Greeks. It begins with the four separate elements, the state of chaos, and ascends by degrees to the three manifestations of Mercurius in the inorganic, organic, and spiritual worlds; and, after attaining the form of Sol and Luna (i.e., the precious metals gold and silver, but also the radiance of the gods who can overcome the strife of the elements by love), it culminates in the one and indivisible (incorruptible, ethereal, eternal) nature of the *anima*, the *quinta essentia, aqua permanens,* tincture, or *lapis philosophorum*. This progression from the number 4 to 3 to 2 to 1 is the "axiom of Maria," which runs in various forms through the whole of alchemy like a *leitmotiv*. If we set aside the numerous "chemical" explanations we come to the following symbolical ground-plan: the initial state of wholeness is marked by four mutually antagonistic tendencies—4 being the minimum number by which a circle can be naturally and visibly defined. The reduction of this number aims at final unity. The first to appear in the progression is the number 3, a masculine number, and out of it comes the feminine number 2.[13] Male and female inevitably constellate the idea of sexual union as the means of producing the 1, which is then consistently called the *filius regius* or *filius philosophorum*.

The quaternity [14] is one of the most widespread archetypes and has also proved to be one of the most useful schemata for representing the arrangement of the functions by which the conscious mind takes its bearings.[15] It is like the crossed threads in the telescope of our understanding. The cross formed by the points of the quaternity is no less universal and has in addition

12 Cf. *Aurora consurgens*, I, Ch. IV: "Evil odours and vapours that infect the mind of the laborant." Also Morienus *(Art. aurif.,* II, p. 34): "Hic enim est odor, qui assimilatur odori sepulcrorum. . . ." (For this is the odour that is similar to the stench of the graves . . .).

13 The interpretation of uneven numbers as masculine and of even numbers as feminine is general in alchemy and originated in antiquity.

14 [For the 2nd edn., there has been a change in the sequence of pars. 405–407, in order to place Jung's summarizing statement in what would seem to be its logical position, i.e., present par. 407.—EDITORS.]

15 Cf. Jacobi, *Psychology of C. G. Jung,* Diagrams IV–VII.

the highest possible moral and religious significance for Western man. Similarly the circle, as the symbol of completeness and perfect being, is a widespread expression for heaven, sun, and God; it also expresses the primordial image of man and the soul.[16] Four as the minimal number by which order can be created represents the pluralistic state of the man who has not yet attained inner unity, hence the state of bondage and disunion, of disintegration, and of being torn in different directions—an agonizing, unredeemed state which longs for union, reconciliation, redemption, healing, and wholeness.

The triad appears as "masculine," i.e., as the active resolve or *agens* whose alchemical equivalent is the "upwelling." In relation to it the dyad is "feminine," the receptive, absorbent *patiens,* or the material that still has to be formed and impregnated (*informatio, impraegnatio*). The psychological equivalent of the triad is want, desire, instinct, aggression and determination, whereas the dyad corresponds to the reaction of the psychic system as a whole to the impulse or decision of the conscious mind. This would of course perish of inanition if it did not succeed in overcoming the inertia of the merely natural man and in achieving its object despite his laziness and constant resistance. But by dint of compulsion or persuasion the conscious mind is able to carry through its purpose, and only in the resultant *action* is a man a living whole and a unity ("In the beginning was the deed," as Faust says) [17]—provided that the action is the mature product of a process embracing the whole psyche and not just a spasm or impulse that has the effect of suppressing it.

At bottom, therefore, our symbolical picture is an illustration of the methods and philosophy of alchemy. These are not warranted by the nature of matter as known to the old masters; they can only derive from the *unconscious* psyche. No doubt there was also a certain amount of *conscious* speculation among the alchemists, but this is no hindrance whatever to unconscious projection, for wherever the mind of the investigator de-

16 For the soul as square, circle, or sphere see *Psychology and Alchemy*, pars. 109 and 439, n. 47.

17 The above remarks should be understood only psychologically and not in the moral sense. The "deed" as such is not the essence of the psychic life-process but only a part of it, although a very important part.

46

parts from exact observation of the facts before it and goes its own way, the unconscious *spiritus rector* will take over and lead the mind back to the unchangeable, underlying archetypes, which are then forced into projection by this regression. We are moving here on familiar ground. These things are depicted in the most magnificent images in the last and greatest work of alchemy—Goethe's *Faust*. Goethe is really describing the experience of the alchemist who discovers that what he has projected into the retort is his own darkness, his unredeemed state, his passion, his struggles to reach the goal, i.e., to become what he really is, to fulfil the purpose for which his mother bore him, and, after the peregrinations of a long life full of confusion and error, to become the *filius regius,* son of the supreme mother. Or we can go even further back to the important forerunner of *Faust,* the *Chymical Wedding* of Christian Rosencreutz (1616), which was assuredly known to Goethe.[18] Fundamentally it is the same theme, the same "Axioma Mariae," telling how Rosencreutz is transformed out of his former unenlightened condition and comes to realize that he is related to "royalty." But in keeping with its period (beginning of the seventeenth century), the whole process is far more projected and the withdrawal of the projection into the hero—which in Faust's case turns him into a superman [19]—is only fleetingly hinted at. Yet the psychological process is essentially the same: the becoming aware of those powerful contents which alchemy sensed in the secrets of matter.

The text that follows the picture of the Mercurial Fountain is mainly concerned with the "water" of the art, i.e., mercury. In order to avoid repetition, I would refer the reader to my lecture "The Spirit Mercurius." Here I will only say that this fluid substance, with all its paradoxical qualities, really signifies the unconscious which has been projected into it. The "sea" is its static condition, the "fountain" its activa-

---

[18] Incidentally, Johann Valentin Andreae, the real author of the *Chymical Wedding,* also wrote a Faust drama in Latin entitled *Turbo, sive Moleste et frustra per cuncta divagans ingenium* (1616), the story of a man who knew everything and was finally disappointed, but who found his salvation in the *contemplatio Christi.* The author, a theologian in Württemberg, lived from 1586 to 1654.

[19] I have dealt with this psychological process at length in *Two Essays,* pars. 224f., 380f.

tion, and the "process" its transformation. The integration of unconscious contents is expressed in the idea of the elixir, the *medicina catholica* or *universalis,* the *aurum potabile,* the *cibus sempiternus* (everlasting food), the health-giving fruits of the philosophical tree, the *vinum ardens,* and all the other innumerable synonyms. Some of them are decidedly ominous but no less characteristic, such as *succus lunariae* or *lunatica* (juice of the moon-plant),[20] *aqua Saturni* (note that Saturn is a baleful deity!), poison, scorpion, dragon, son of the fire, boys' or dogs' urine, brimstone, devil, etc.

Although not expressly stated in the text, the gushing up and flowing back of the Mercurial Fountain within its basin completes a circle, and this is an essential characteristic of Mercurius because he is also the serpent that fertilizes, kills, and devours itself and brings itself to birth again. We may mention in this connection that the circular sea with no outlet, which perpetually replenishes itself by means of a spring bubbling up in its centre, is to be found in Nicholas of Cusa as an allegory of God.[21]

[20] An allusion to madness. The *afflictio animae* is mentioned in Olympiodorus (Berthelot, *Alch. grecs*, II, iv, 43). Morienus (*Art. aurif.,* II, p. 18), and Maier (*Symb. aur. mens.,* p. 568), and in Chinese alchemy (Wei Po-yang, "An Ancient Chinese Treatise," pp. 241–45).

[21] God is the source, river, and sea which all contain the same water. The Trinity is a life that "proceeds from itself to itself, by way of itself"—Vansteenberghe, *Le Cardinal Nicolas de Cues,* pp. 296f.

KING AND QUEEN

The *arcanum artis,* or *coniunctio Solis et Lunae* as supreme union of hostile opposites, was not shown in our first picture; but now it is illustrated in considerable detail, as its importance deserves, in a series of pictures. King and Queen, bridegroom and bride, approach one another for the purpose of betrothal or marriage. The incest element appears in the brother-sister relationship of Apollo and Diana. The pair of them stand respectively on sun and moon, thus indicating their solar and lunar nature in accordance with the astrological assumption of the importance of the sun's position for man and the moon's for woman. The meeting is somewhat distant at first, as the court clothes suggest. The two give each other their *left* hands, and this can hardly be unintentional since it is contrary to custom. The gesture points to a closely guarded secret, to the "left-hand path," as the Indian Tantrists call their Shiva and Shakti worship. The left-hand (sinister) side is the dark, the unconscious side. The left is inauspicious and awkward; also it is the side of the heart, from which comes not only love but all the evil thoughts connected with it, the moral contradictions in human nature that are expressed most clearly in our affective life. The contact of left hands could therefore be taken as an indication of the affective nature of the relationship, of its dubious character, since this is a mixture of "heavenly and earthly" love further complicated by an incestuous *sous-entendu.* In this delicate yet altogether human situation the gesture of the *right* hands strikes us as compensatory. They are holding a device composed of five $(4 + 1)$ flowers. The branches in the hands each have two flowers; these four again refer to the four elements of which two—fire and air—are active and two—water and earth—passive, the former being ascribed to the man and the latter to the woman. The fifth flower comes from above and presumably represents the *quinta essentia;* it is brought by the dove of the Holy Ghost, an analogy of Noah's dove that carried the olive branch of reconciliation in its beak. The bird descends from the quintessential star (cf. fig. 1).

The real secret lies in the union of *right* hands, for, as the picture shows, this is mediated by the *donum Spiritus Sancti*, the royal art. The "sinister" left-handed contact here becomes associated with the union, effected from above, of two quaternities (the masculine and feminine manifestations of the four elements) in the form of an ogdoad consisting of five flowers and three branches. These masculine numbers point to action, decision, purpose, and movement. The fifth flower is distinguished from the four in that it is brought by the dove. The three branches correspond to the upwelling of Mercurius *triplex nomine* or to the three pipes of the fountain. So once again we have an abbreviated recapitulation of the *opus*, i.e., of its deeper meaning as shown in the first picture. The text to Figure 2 begins significantly with the words: "Mark well, in the art of our magisterium nothing is concealed by the philosophers except the secret of the art which may not be revealed to all and sundry. For were that to happen, that man would be accursed; he would incur the wrath of God and perish of the apoplexy. Wherefore all error in the art arises because men do not begin with the proper substance,[1] and for this reason you should employ venerable Nature, because from her and through her and in her is our art born and in naught else: and so our magisterium is the work of Nature and not of the worker."[2]

If we take the fear of divine punishment for betrayal at its face value, the reason for this must lie in something that is thought to endanger the soul's salvation, i.e., a typical "peril of the soul." The causal "wherefore" with which the next sentence begins can only refer to the secret that must not be revealed; but because the *prima materia* remains unknown in consequence, all those who do not know the secret fall into error,

---

[1] *Debita materia*, meaning the *prima materia* of the process.

[2] *Rosarium*, p. 219: "Nota bene: In arte nostri magisterii nihil est celatum a Philosophis excepto secreto artis, quod non licet cuiquam revelare: quodsi fieret, ille malediceretur et indignationem Domini incurreret et apoplexia moreretur. Quare omnis error in arte existit ex eo quod debitam materiam non accipiunt. Igitur venerabili utimini natura, quia ex ea et per eam et in ea generatur ars nostra et non in alio: et ideo magisterium nostrum est opus naturae et non opificis."

Nota bene: In arte noſtri magiſterij nihil eſt ~Secretum~
celatũ à Philoſophis excepto ſecreto artis, quod ~artis~
non licet cuiquam reuelare, quod ſi fieret ille ma
lediceretur , & indignationem domini incurreret , & apoplexia moreretur. ☞ Quare omnis error in arte exiſtit , ex eo, quod debitam

C ij

Figure 2

and this happens because, as said, they choose something arbitrary and artificial instead of pure Nature. The emphasis laid on *venerabilis natura* [3] gives us some idea of that passion for investigation which ultimately gave birth to natural science, but which so often proved inimical to faith. Worship of nature, a legacy from the past, stood in more or less secret opposition to the views of the Church and led the mind and heart in the direction of a "left-hand path." What a sensation Petrarch's ascent of Mont Ventoux caused! St. Augustine had warned in his *Confessions* (X, viii): "And men go forth to admire the high mountains and the great waves of the sea and the broad torrent of the rivers and the vast expanse of the ocean and the orbits of the stars, and to turn away from themselves. . . ."

The exclusive emphasis on nature as the one and only basis of the art is in flagrant contrast to the ever-recurring protestation that the art is a *donum Spiritus Sancti,* an arcanum of the *sapientia Dei,* and so forth, from which we would have to conclude that the alchemists were unshakably orthodox in their beliefs. I do not think that this can be doubted as a rule. On the contrary, their belief in illumination through the Holy Ghost seems to have been a psychological necessity in view of the ominous darkness of nature's secrets.

Now if a text which insists so much on pure nature is explained or illustrated by a picture like Figure 2, we must assume that the relationship between king and queen was taken to be something perfectly natural. Meditation and speculation about the mystery of the *coniunctio* were inevitable, and this would certainly not leave erotic fantasy untouched, if only because these symbolical pictures spring from the corresponding unconscious contents—half spiritual, half sexual—and are also intended to remind us of that twilit region, for only from indistinguishable night can the light be born. This is what nature and natural experience teach, but the spirit believes in the *lumen de lumine*—the light born of light.[4] Somehow the artifex was entangled in this game of unconscious projection and was

---

[3] Ruska, *Turba,* Sermo XXIX, p. 137.

[4] Cf. *Aurora consurgens,* I, where the parables "Of the Black Earth," "Of the Flood of Waters and of Death," "Of the Babylonish Captivity," are followed by the parable "Of the Philosophic Faith" with its avowal of the *lumen de lumine.* Cf. also Avicenna, "Declaratio lapidis physici," *Theatr. chem.,* IV, p. 990.

bound to experience the mysterious happening with shudders of fear, as a *tremendum*. Even that scoffer and blasphemer Agrippa von Nettesheim displays a remarkable reticence in his criticism of "Alkumistica." [5] After saying a great deal about this dubious art, he adds: [6] "Permulta adhuc de hoc arte (mihi tamen non ad modum inimica) dicere possem, nisi iuratum esset (quod facere solent, qui mysteriis initiantur) de silentio" (I could say much more about this art—which I do not find so disagreeable—were it not for the oath of silence usually taken by initiates into mysteries).[7] Such a mitigation of his criticism, most unexpected in Agrippa, makes one think that he is on the defensive: somehow he was impressed by the royal art.

It is not necessary to think of the secret of the art as anything very lurid. Nature knows nothing of moral squalor, indeed her truths are alarming enough. We need only bear in mind one fact: that the desired *coniunctio* was not a legitimate union but was always—one could almost say, on principle—incestuous. The fear that surrounds this complex—the "fear of incest"—is quite typical and has already been stressed by Freud. It is further exacerbated by fear of the compulsive force which emanates from most unconscious contents.

The left-handed contact and crosswise union of the right hands—*sub rosa*—is a startlingly concrete and yet very subtle hint of the delicate situation in which "venerable nature" has placed the adept. Although the Rosicrucian movement cannot be traced further back than the *Fama* and *Confessio fraternitatis*

5 A corruption of "alchymia."

6 *De incertitudine et vanitate omnium scientiarum*, Ch. XC.

7 Later, Agrippa (ibid.) says one or two other things about the stone: "As to that unique and blessed substance, besides which there is no other although you may find it everywhere, as to that most sacred stone of the philosophers—almost I had broken my oath and made myself a desecrator of temples by blurting out its name —I shall nevertheless speak in circumlocutions and dark hints, so that none but the sons of the art and the initiates of this mystery shall understand. The thing is one which has neither too fiery nor too earthen a substance. . . . More I am not permitted to say, and yet there be greater things than these. However, I consider this art—with which I have a certain familiarity—as being the most worthy of that honour which Thucydides pays to an upright woman, when he says that the best is she of whom least is said either in praise or blame." Concerning the oath of secrecy, see also Senior, *De chemia*, p. 92: "Hoc est secretum, super quo iuraverunt, quod non indicarent in aliquo libro" (This is the secret which they promised on oath not to divulge in any book).

of Andreae at the beginning of the seventeenth century,[8] we are nevertheless confronted with a "rosie cross" in this curious bouquet of three flowering branches, which evidently originated sometime before 1550 but, equally obviously, makes no claim to be a true *rosicrux*.[9] As we have already said, its threefold structure is reminiscent of the Mercurial Fountain, while at the same time it points to the important fact that the "rose" is the product of three *living* things: the king, the queen, and between them the dove of the Holy Ghost. Mercurius *triplex nomine* is thus converted into three figures, and he can no longer be thought of as a metal or mineral, but only as "spirit." In this form also he is triple-natured—masculine, feminine, and divine. His coincidence with the Holy Ghost as the third person of the Trinity certainly has no foundation in dogma, but "venerable nature" evidently enabled the alchemist to provide the Holy Ghost with a most unorthodox and distinctly earth-bound partner, or rather to complement him with that divine spirit which had been imprisoned in all creatures since the day of Creation. This "lower" spirit is the Primordial Man, hermaphroditic by nature and of Iranian origin, who was imprisoned in Physis.[10] He is the spherical, i.e., perfect, man who appears at the beginning and end of time and is man's own beginning and end. He is man's totality, which is beyond the division of the sexes and can only be reached when male and female come together in one. The revelation of this higher meaning solves the problems created by the "sinister" contact and produces from the chaotic darkness the *lumen quod superat omnia lumina*.

If I did not know from ample experience that such developments also occur in modern man, who cannot possibly be suspected of having any knowledge of the Gnostic doctrine of the Anthropos, I should be inclined to think that the alchemists were keeping up a secret tradition, although the evidence for this (the hints contained in the writings of Zosimos of

8 Both texts are supposed to have been in circulation in manuscript from about 1610, according to F. Maack, editor of Rosencreutz's *Chymische Hochzeit*, pp. xxxviif. [They are to be found there at pp. 47–84.—EDITORS.]

9 A kind of "rosie cross" can also be seen in Luther's crest.

10 Cf. *Psychology and Alchemy*, par. 436, and Reitzenstein and Schaeder, *Studien zum antiken Synkretismus*.

Panopolis) is so scanty that Waite, who knows medieval alchemy relatively well, doubts whether a secret tradition existed at all.[11] I am therefore of the opinion, based on my professional work, that the Anthropos idea in medieval alchemy was largely "autochthonous," i.e., the outcome of subjective experience. It is an "eternal" idea, an archetype that can appear spontaneously at any time and in any place. We meet the Anthropos even in ancient Chinese alchemy, in the writings of Wei Po-yang, about A.D. 142. There he is called *chên-jên* ('true man').[12]

The revelation of the Anthropos is associated with no ordinary religious emotion; it signifies much the same thing as the vision of Christ for the believing Christian. Nevertheless it does not appear *ex opere divino* but *ex opere naturae;* not from above but from the transformation of a shade from Hades, akin to evil itself and bearing the name of the pagan god of revelation. This dilemma throws a new light on the secret of the art: the very serious danger of heresy. Consequently the alchemists found themselves between Scylla and Charybdis: on the one hand they ran the conscious risk of being misunderstood and suspected of fraudulent gold-making, and on the other of being burned at the stake as heretics. As to the gold, right at the beginning of the text to Figure 2, the *Rosarium* quotes the words of Senior: "Aurum nostrum non est aurum vulgi." But, as history shows, the alchemist would rather risk being suspected of gold-making than of heresy. It is still an open question, which perhaps can never be answered, how far the alchemist was conscious of the true nature of his art. Even texts as revealing as the *Rosarium* and *Aurora consurgens* do not help us in this respect.

As regards the psychology of this picture, we must stress above all else that it depicts a human encounter where love plays the decisive part. The conventional dress of the pair suggests an equally conventional attitude in both of them. Convention still separates them and hides their natural reality, but the crucial contact of left hands points to something "sinister," illegitimate, morganatic, emotional, and instinctive, i.e., the fatal touch of incest and its "perverse" fascination. At the same time the intervention of the Holy Ghost reveals the hidden meaning

11 Waite, *The Secret Tradition.*
12 Wei Po-yang, p. 241.

of the incest, whether of brother and sister or of mother and son, as a repulsive symbol for the *unio mystica*. Although the union of close blood-relatives is everywhere taboo, it is yet the prerogative of kings (witness the incestuous marriages of the Pharaohs, etc.). Incest symbolizes union with one's own being, it means individuation or becoming a self, and, because this is so vitally important, it exerts an unholy fascination—not, perhaps, as a crude reality, but certainly as a psychic process controlled by the unconscious, a fact well known to anybody who is familiar with psychopathology. It is for this reason, and not because of occasional cases of human incest, that the first gods were believed to propagate their kind incestuously. Incest is simply the union of like with like, which is the next stage in the development of the primitive idea of self-fertilization.[13]

This psychological situation sums up what we can all see for ourselves if we analyse a transference carefully. The conventional meeting is followed by an unconscious "familiarization" of one's partner, brought about by the projection of archaic, infantile fantasies which were originally vested in members of the patient's own family and which, because of their positive or negative fascination, attach him to parents, brothers, and sisters.[14] The transference of these fantasies to the doctor draws him into the atmosphere of family intimacy, and although this is the last thing he wants, it nevertheless provides a workable *prima materia*. Once the transference has appeared, the doctor must accept it as part of the treatment and try to understand it, otherwise it will be just another piece of neurotic stupidity. The transference itself is a perfectly natural phenomenon which does not by any means happen only in the consulting-room—it can be seen everywhere and may lead to all sorts of nonsense, like all unrecognized projections. Medical treatment of the transference gives the patient a priceless opportunity to withdraw his projections, to make good his losses, and

[13] The union of "like with like" in the form of homosexual relationships is to be found in the "Visio Arislei" (*Art. aurif.*, I, p. 147), marking the stage preceding the brother-sister incest.

[14] According to Freud, these projections are infantile wish-fantasies. But a more thorough examination of neuroses in childhood shows that such fantasies are largely dependent on the psychology of the parents, that is, are caused by the parents' wrong attitude to the child. Cf. "Analytical Psychology and Education," pars. 216ff.

to integrate his personality. The impulses underlying it certainly show their dark side to begin with, however much one may try to whitewash them; for an integral part of the work is the *umbra solis* or *sol niger* of the alchemists, the black shadow which everybody carries with him, the inferior and therefore hidden aspect of the personality, the weakness that goes with every strength, the night that follows every day, the evil in the good.[15] The realization of this fact is naturally coupled with the danger of falling victim to the shadow, but the danger also brings with it the possibility of consciously deciding not to become its victim. A visible enemy is always better than an invisible one. In this case I can see no advantage whatever in behaving like an ostrich. It is certainly no ideal for people always to remain childish, to live in a perpetual state of delusion about themselves, foisting everything they dislike on to their neighbours and plaguing them with their prejudices and projections. How many marriages are wrecked for years, and sometimes forever, because he sees his mother in his wife and she her father in her husband, and neither ever recognizes the other's reality! Life has difficulties enough without that; we might at least spare ourselves the stupidest of them. But, without a fundamental discussion of the situation, it is often simply impossible to break these infantile projections. As this is the legitimate aim and real meaning of the transference, it inevitably leads, whatever method of rapprochement be used, to discussion and understanding and hence to a heightened consciousness, which is a measure of the personality's integration. During this discussion the conventional disguises are dropped and the true man comes to light. He is in very truth reborn from this psychological relationship, and his field of consciousness is rounded into a circle.

It would be quite natural to suppose that the king and queen represent a transference relationship in which the king stands for the masculine partner and the queen for the feminine partner. But this is by no means the case, because the figures represent contents which have been projected from the unconscious of the adept (and his *soror mystica*). Now the adept

---

15 Hence *Aurora consurgens*, I, Ch. VI, says: ". . . and all my bones are troubled before the face of my iniquity." Cf. Ps. 37 : 4 (D.V.): ". . . there is no peace for my bones, because of my sins."

is conscious of himself as a man, consequently his masculinity cannot be projected, since this only happens to unconscious contents. As it is primarily a question of man and woman here, the projected fragment of personality can only be the feminine component of the man, i.e., his anima.[16] Similarly, in the woman's case, only the masculine component can be projected. There is thus a curious counter-crossing of the sexes: the man (in this case the adept) is represented by the queen, and the woman (the *soror mystica*) by the king. It seems to me that the flowers forming the "symbol" suggest this counter-crossing. The reader should therefore bear in mind that the picture shows two archetypal figures meeting, and that Luna is secretly in league with the adept, and Sol with his woman helper. The fact that the figures are royal expresses, like real royalty, their archetypal character; they are collective figures common to large numbers of people. If the main ingredient of this mystery were the enthronement of a king or the deification of a mortal, then the figure of the king might possibly be a projection and would in that case correspond to the adept. But the subsequent development of the drama has quite another meaning, so we can discount this possibility.[17]

The fact that, for reasons which can be proved empirically, king and queen play cross roles and represent the unconscious

---

[16] Cf. *Two Essays*, pars. 296ff. [Also "Concerning the Archetypes, with Special Reference to the Anima Concept" and *Aion*, ch. 3.—EDITORS.]

[17] It may be helpful to remind the reader that in Rider Haggard's *She* there is a description of this "royal" figure. Leo Vincey, the hero, is young and handsome, the acme of perfection, a veritable Apollo. Beside him there stands his fatherly guardian, Holly, whose resemblance to a baboon is described in great detail. But inwardly Holly is a paragon of wisdom and moral rectitude—even his name hints at "holy." In spite of their banality both of them have superhuman qualities, Leo as well as the devout "baboon." (Together they correspond to the *sol et umbra eius*.) The third figure is the faithful servant who bears the significant name of Job. He stands for the long-suffering but loyal companion who has to endure both superhuman perfection and subhuman baboonishness. Leo may be regarded as the sun-god; he goes in quest of "She" who "dwells among the tombs" and who is reputed to kill her lovers one by one—a characteristic also ascribed by Benoît to his "Atlantide"—and to rejuvenate herself by periodically bathing in a pillar of fire. "She" stands for Luna, and particularly for the dangerous new moon. (It is at the *synodus* of the *novilunium*—i.e., at the *coniunctio* of the Sun and Moon at the time of the new moon—that the bride kills her lover.) The story eventually leads, in *Ayesha*, another novel of Haggard's, to the mystical hierosgamos.

contra-sexual side of the adept and his soror leads to a painful complication which by no means simplifies the problem of transference. Scientific integrity, however, forbids all simplification of situations that are not simple, as is obviously the case here. The pattern of relationship is simple enough, but, when it comes to detailed description in any given case, it is extremely difficult to make out from which angle the relationship is being described and what aspect we are describing. The pattern is as follows:

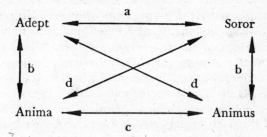

The direction of the arrows indicates the pull from masculine to feminine and *vice versa,* and from the unconscious of one person to the conscious of the other, thus denoting a positive transference relationship. The following relationships have therefore to be distinguished, although in certain cases they can all merge into each other, and this naturally leads to the greatest possible confusion:

(a) An uncomplicated personal relationship.

(b) A relationship of the man to his anima and of the woman to her animus.

(c) A relationship of anima to animus and *vice versa.*

(d) A relationship of the woman's animus to the man (which happens when the woman is identical with her animus), and of the man's anima to the woman (which happens when the man is identical with his anima).

In describing the transference problem with the help of this series of illustrations, I have not always kept these different possibilities apart; for in real life they are invariably mixed up and it would have put an intolerable strain on the explanation had I attempted a rigidly schematic exposition. Thus the king and queen each display every conceivable shade of meaning from the superhuman to the subhuman, sometimes appearing as a transcendental figure, sometimes hiding in the figure of the adept. The reader should bear this in mind if he comes across any real or supposed contradictions in the remarks which follow.

These counter-crossing transference relationships are foreshadowed in folklore: the archetype of the cross-marriage, which I call the "marriage quaternio," [18] can also be found in fairytales. An Icelandic fairytale [19] tells the following story:

Finna was a girl with mysterious powers. One day, when her father was setting out for the Althing, she begged him to refuse any suitor who might ask for her hand. There were many suitors present, but the father refused them all. On the way home he met a strange man, Geir by name, who forced the father at point of sword to promise his daughter to him. So they were married, and Finna took Sigurd her brother with her to her new home. About Christmas-time, when Finna was busy with the festive preparations, Geir disappeared. Finna and her brother went out to look for him and found him on an island with a beautiful woman. After Christmas, Geir suddenly appeared in Finna's bedroom. In the bed lay a child. Geir asked her whose child it was, and Finna answered that it was her child. And so it happened for three years in succession, and each time Finna accepted the child. But at the third time, Geir was released from his spell. The beautiful woman on the island was Ingeborg, his sister. Geir had disobeyed his stepmother, a witch, and she had laid a curse on him: he was to have three children by his sister, and unless he found a wife who knew everything and held her peace, he would be changed into a snake and his sister into a filly. Geir was saved by the conduct of his wife; and he married his sister Ingeborg to Sigurd.

Another example is the Russian fairytale "Prince Danila Govorila." [20] There is a young prince who is given a lucky ring by a witch. But its magic will work only on one condition: he must marry none but the girl whose finger the ring fits.

[18] The alchemical pairs of opposites are often arranged in such quaternios, as I shall show in a later work. [Cf. *Mysterium Coniunctionis*, pars. 5ff., and *Aion*, pars. 394ff.—EDITORS.]

[19] Naumann (ed.), *Isländische Volksmärchen*, No. 8, pp. 47ff.

[20] Guterman (trans.), *Russian Fairy Tales*, pp. 351ff.

When he grows up he goes in search of a bride, but all in vain, because the ring fits none of them. So he laments his fate to his sister, who asks to try on the ring. It fits perfectly. Thereupon her brother wants to marry her, but she thinks it would be a sin and sits at the door of the house weeping. Some old beggars who are passing comfort her and give her the following advice: "Make four dolls and put them in the four corners of the room. If your brother summons you to the wedding, go, but if he summons you to the bedchamber, do not hurry! Trust in God and follow our advice."

After the wedding her brother summons her to bed. Then the four dolls begin to sing:

> Cuckoo, Prince Danila,
> Cuckoo, Govorila,
> Cuckoo, he takes his sister,
> Cuckoo, for a wife,
> Cuckoo, earth open wide,
> Cuckoo, sister fall inside.

The earth opens and swallows her up. Her brother calls her three times, but by the third time she has already vanished. She goes along under the earth until she comes to the hut of Baba Yaga,[21] whose daughter kindly shelters her and hides her from the witch. But before long the witch discovers her and heats up the oven. The two girls then seize the old woman and put her in the oven instead, thus escaping the witch's persecution. They reach the prince's castle, where the sister is recognized by her brother's servant. But her brother cannot tell the two girls apart, they are so alike. So the servant advises him to make a test: the prince is to fill a skin with blood and put it under his arm. The servant will then stab him in the side with a knife and the prince is to fall down as if dead. The sister will then surely betray herself. And so it happens: the sister throws herself upon him with a great cry, whereupon the prince springs up and embraces her. But the magic ring also fits the finger of the witch's daughter, so the prince marries her and gives his sister to a suitable husband.

In this tale the incest is on the point of being committed, but is prevented by the peculiar ritual with the four dolls. The

[21] The Russian arch-witch.

four dolls in the four corners of the room form the marriage quaternio, the aim being to prevent the incest by putting four in place of two. The four dolls form a magic simulacrum which stops the incest by removing the sister to the underworld, where she discovers her alter ego. Thus we can say that the witch who gave the young prince the fatal ring was his mother-in-law-to-be, for, as a witch, she must certainly have known that the ring would fit not only his sister but her own daughter.

In both tales the incest is an evil fate that cannot easily be avoided. Incest, as an endogamous relationship, is an expression of the libido which serves to hold the family together. One could therefore define it as "kinship libido," a kind of instinct which, like a sheep-dog, keeps the family group intact. This form of libido is the diametrical opposite of the exogamous form. The two forms together hold each other in check: the endogamous form tends towards the sister and the exogamous form towards some stranger. The best compromise is therefore a first cousin. There is no hint of this in our fairy-stories, but the marriage quaternio is clear enough. In the Icelandic story we have the schema:

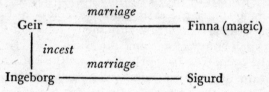

In the Russian:

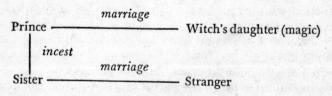

The two schemata agree in a remarkable way. In both cases the hero wins a bride who has something to do with magic or the world beyond. Assuming that the archetype of the marriage quaternio described above is at the bottom of these folkloristic quaternities, the stories are obviously based on the following schema:

62

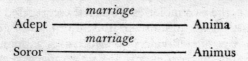

Marriage with the anima is the psychological equivalent of absolute identity between conscious and unconscious. But since such a condition is possible only in the complete absence of psychological self-knowledge, it must be more or less primitive, i.e., the man's relationship to the woman is essentially an anima projection. The only sign that the whole thing is unconscious is the remarkable fact that the carrier of the anima-image is distinguished by magical characteristics. These characteristics are missing from the soror-animus relationship in the stories; that is, the unconscious does not make itself felt at all as a separate experience. From this we must conclude that the symbolism of the stories rests on a much more primitive mental structure than the alchemical quaternio and its psychological equivalent. Therefore we must expect that on a still more primitive level the anima too will lose her magical attributes, the result being an uncomplicated, purely matter-of-fact marriage quaternio. And we do find a parallel to the two crossed pairs in the so-called "cross-cousin marriage." In order to explain this primitive form of marriage I must go into some detail. The marriage of a man's sister to his wife's brother is a relic of the "sister-exchange marriage" characteristic of the structure of many primitive tribes. But at the same time this double marriage is the primitive parallel of the problem which concerns us here: the conscious and unconscious dual relationship between adept and soror on the one hand and king and queen (or animus and anima) on the other. John Layard's important study, "The Incest Taboo and the Virgin Archetype," put me in mind of the sociological aspects of our psychologem. The primitive tribe falls into two halves, of which Howitt says: "It is upon the division of the whole community into two exogamous intermarrying classes that the whole social structure is built up." [22] These "moieties" show themselves in the lay-out of settlements [23] as well as in many strange customs. At ceremonies,

[22] *The Native Tribes of S.E. Australia*, p. 157; cf. Frazer, *Totemism and Exogamy*, I, p. 306.
[23] Layard, *Stone Men of Malekula*, pp. 62ff.

for instance, the two moieties are strictly segregated and neither may trespass on the other's territory. Even when going out on a hunt, they at once divide into two halves as soon as they set up camp, and the two camps are so arranged that there is a natural obstacle between them, e.g., the bed of a stream. On the other hand the two halves are connected by what Hocart calls "the ritual interdependence of the two sides" or "mutual ministration." In New Guinea one side breeds and fattens pigs and dogs, not for themselves but for the other side, and vice versa. Or when there is a death in the village and the funeral feast is prepared, this is eaten by the other side, and so on.[24] [Another form of such division elsewhere is] [25] the widespread institution of "dual kingship." [26]

The names given to the two sides are particularly enlightening, such as—to mention only a few—east and west, high and low, day and night, male and female, water and land, left and right. It is not difficult to see from these names that the two halves are felt to be antithetical and thus the expression of an endopsychic antithesis. The antithesis can be formulated as the masculine ego versus the feminine "other," i.e., conscious versus unconscious personified as anima. The primary splitting of the psyche into conscious and unconscious seems to be the cause of the division within the tribe and the settlement. It is a division founded on fact but not consciously recognized as such.

The social split is by origin a matrilineal division into two, but in reality it represents a division of the tribe and settlement into four. The quartering comes about through the crossing of the matrilineal by a patrilineal line of division, [so that the entire population is divided into patrilineal as well as matrilineal moieties].[27] The practical purpose of this quartering is the separation and differentiation of marriage classes, [or "kinship sections," as they are now called]. The basic pattern is a square or circle divided by a cross; it forms the ground-plan of the primitive settlement and the archaic city, also of monas-

[24] Hocart, *Kings and Councillors*, p. 265.

[25] [Pars. 433ff. incorporate corrections made by Dr. John Layard in 1955 with reference to his own writings and authorized by Jung in the 1958 Swiss edition. Later corrections made by Dr. Layard (1965) are given in square brackets.—EDITORS.]

[26] Ibid., pp. 157, 193.

[27] Layard, *Stone Men of Malekula*, pp. 85ff.

teries, convents, etc., as can be seen in Europe, Asia, and pre-historic America.[28] The Egyptian hieroglyph for "city" is a St. Andrew's cross in a circle.[29]

In specifying the marriage classes, it should be mentioned that every man belongs to his father's patrilineal moiety, [and the woman he marries must not come from his mother's moiety. In other words, he can take a wife only from the opposite matrilineal *and* patrilineal moiety.] In order to avoid the possibility of incest, he marries his mother's brother's daughter and gives his sister to his wife's brother (sister-exchange marriage). This results in the cross-cousin marriage.[30]

This form of union, consisting of two brother-and-sister marriages crossing each other, seems to be the original model for the peculiar psychologem which we find in alchemy:

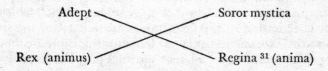

Adept ——————— Soror mystica

Rex (animus) ——————— Regina [31] (anima)

When I say "model" I do not mean that the system of marriage classes was the cause and our psychologem the effect. I merely wish to point out that this system predated the alchemical quaternio. Nor can we assume that the primitive marriage quaternio is the absolute origin of this archetype, for the latter is not a human invention at all but a fact that existed long before consciousness, as is true of all ritual symbols among primitives as well as among civilized peoples today. We do certain things simply without thinking, because they have always been done like that.[32]

The difference between the primitive and the cultural marriage quaternio consists in the fact that the former is a sociological and the latter a mystical phenomenon. While marriage

[28] Hocart, *Kings and Councillors*, pp. 244ff.

[29] Ibid., p. 250.

[30] Layard, "The Incest Taboo," pp. 270ff.

[31] I would remind the reader that Rex and Regina are usually brother and sister or sometimes mother and son.

[32] If we think at all when doing these things, it must be a preconscious or rather an unconscious act of thought. Psychological explanations cannot very well get on without such an hypothesis.

classes have all but disappeared among civilized peoples, they nevertheless re-emerge on a higher cultural level as spiritual ideas. In the interests of the welfare and development of the tribe, the exogamous social order thrust the endogamous tendency into the background so as to prevent the danger of regression to a state of having no groups at all. It insisted on the introduction of "new blood" both physically and spiritually, and it thus proved to be a powerful instrument in the development of culture. In the words of Spencer and Gillen: "This system of what has been called group marriage, serving as it does to bind more or less closely together groups of individuals who are mutually interested in one another's welfare, has been one of the most powerful agents in the early stages of the upward development of the human race." [33] Layard has amplified this idea in his above-mentioned study. He regards the endogamous (incest) tendency as a genuine instinct which, if denied realization in the flesh, must realize itself in the spirit. Just as the exogamous order made culture possible in the first place, so also it contains a latent spiritual purpose. Layard says: "Its latent or spiritual purpose is to enlarge the spiritual horizon by developing the idea that there is after all a sphere in which the primary desire may be satisfied, namely the divine sphere of the gods together with that of their semi-divine counterparts, the culture heroes." [34] The idea of the incestuous hierosgamos does in fact appear in the civilized religions and blossoms forth in the supreme spirituality of Christian imagery (Christ and the Church, *sponsus* and *sponsa*, the mysticism of the Song of Songs, etc.). "Thus the incest taboo," says Layard, "leads in full circle out of the biological sphere into the spiritual." [35] On the primitive level the feminine image, the anima, is still completely unconscious and therefore in a state of latent projection. Through the differentiation of the "four-class marriage system" into the eight-class,[36] the degree of kinship between marriage partners is considerably diluted, and in the twelve-class system it becomes [further reduced]. These "dichotomies" [37] obviously serve to

---

[33] *The Northern Tribes of Central Australia*, p. 74.

[34] Layard, "The Incest Taboo," p. 284.　　[35] Ibid., p. 293.

[36] In this system a man marries his [mother's mother's brother's daughter's daughter].

[37] Hocart, *Kings and Councillors*, p. 259.

enlarge the framework of the marriage classes and thus to draw more and more groups of people into the kinship system. Naturally such an enlargement was possible only where a sizeable population was expanding.[38] The eight-class and particularly the twelve-class systems mean a great advance for the exogamous order, but an equally severe repression of the endogamous tendency, which is thereby stimulated to a new advance in its turn. Whenever an instinctive force—i.e., a certain sum of psychic energy—is driven into the background through a one-sided (in this case, exogamous) attitude on the part of the conscious mind, it leads to a dissociation of personality. The conscious personality with its one-track (exogamous) tendency comes up against an invisible (endogamous) opponent, and because this is unconscious it is felt to be a stranger and therefore manifests itself in projected form. At first it makes its appearance in human figures who have the power to do what others may not do—kings and princes, for example. This is probably the reason for the royal incest prerogative, as in ancient Egypt. To the extent that the magical power of royalty was derived increasingly from the gods, the incest prerogative shifted to the latter and so gave rise to the incestuous hierosgamos. But when the numinous aura surrounding the person of the king is taken over by the gods, it has been transferred to a spiritual authority, which results in the projection of an autonomous psychic complex—in other words, psychic existence becomes reality. Thus Layard logically derives the anima from the numen of the goddess.[39] In the shape of the goddess the anima is manifestly projected, but in her proper (psychological) shape she is *introjected;* she is, as Layard says, the "anima within." She is the natural *sponsa,* man's mother or sister or daughter or wife from the beginning, the companion whom the endogamous tendency vainly seeks to win in the form of mother and sister. She represents that longing which has always had to be sacrificed since the grey dawn of history. Layard therefore speaks very rightly of "internalization through sacrifice." [40]

The endogamous tendency finds an outlet in the exalted

---

[38] In China, for instance, one can still find vestiges of the twelve-class system.

[39] Layard, "The Incest Taboo," pp. 281ff.

[40] Ibid., p. 284. Perhaps I may point out the similar conclusions reached in *Symbols of Transformation,* pars. 464ff.

sphere of the gods and in the higher world of the spirit. Here it shows itself to be an instinctive force of a spiritual nature; and, regarded in this light, the life of the spirit on the highest level is a return to the beginnings, so that man's development becomes a recapitulation of the stages that lead ultimately to the perfection of life in the spirit.

The specifically alchemical projection looks at first sight like a regression: god and goddess are reduced to king and queen, and these in turn look like mere allegories of chemical substances which are about to combine. But the regression is only apparent. In reality it is a highly remarkable development: the conscious mind of the medieval investigator was still under the influence of metaphysical ideas, but because he could not derive them from nature he projected them into nature. He sought for them in matter, because he supposed that they were most likely to be found there. It was really a question of a transference of numen the converse of that from the king to the god. The numen seemed to have migrated in some mysterious way from the world of the spirit to the realm of matter. But the descent of the projection into matter had led some of the old alchemists, for example Morienus Romanus, to the clear realization that this matter was not just the human body (or something in it) but the human personality itself. These prescient masters had already got beyond the inevitable stage of obtuse materialism that had yet to be born from the womb of time. But it was not until the discoveries of modern psychology that this human "matter" of the alchemists could be recognized as the *psyche.*

On the psychological level, the tangle of relationships in the cross-cousin marriage reappears in the transference problem. The dilemma here consists in the fact that anima and animus are projected upon their human counterparts and thus create by suggestion a primitive relationship which evidently goes back to the time of group marriages. But in so far as anima and animus undoubtedly represent the contrasexual components of the personality, their kinship character does not point backwards to the group marriage but "forwards" to the integration of personality, i.e., to individuation.

Our present-day civilization with its cult of consciousness— if this can be called civilization—has a Christian stamp, which means that neither anima nor animus is integrated but is still in the state of projection, i.e., expressed by dogma. On this level both these figures are unconscious as components of personality, though their effectiveness is still apparent in the numinous aura surrounding the dogmatic ideas of bridegroom and bride. Our "civilization," however, has turned out to be a very doubtful proposition, a distinct falling away from the lofty ideal of Christianity; and, in consequence, the projections have largely fallen away from the divine figures and have necessarily settled in the human sphere. This is understandable enough, since the "enlightened" intellect cannot imagine anything greater than man except those tin gods with totalitarian pretensions who call themselves State or Fuehrer. This regression has made itself as plain as could be wished in Germany and other countries. And even where it is not so apparent, the lapsed projections have a disturbing effect on human relationships and wreck at least a quarter of the marriages. If we decline to measure the vicissitudes of the world's history by the standards of right and wrong, true and false, good and evil, but prefer to see the retrograde step in every advance, the evil in every good, the error in every truth, we might compare the present regression with the apparent retreat which led from scholasticism to the mystical trend of natural philosophy and thence to materialism. Just as materialism led to empirical science and thus to a new understanding of the psyche, so the totalitarian psychosis with its frightful consequences and the intolerable disturbance of human relationships are forcing us to pay attention to the psyche and our abysmal unconsciousness of it. Never before has mankind as a whole experienced the numen of the psychological factor on so vast a scale. In one sense this is a catastrophe and a retrogression without parallel, but it is not beyond the bounds of possibility that such an experience also has its positive aspects and might become the seed of a nobler culture in a regenerated age. It is possible that the endogamous urge is not ultimately tending towards projection at all; it may be trying to unite the different components of the personality on the pattern of the cross-cousin marriage, but on a higher plane where "spiritual marriage" becomes an inner experience that is not projected. Such an experience has long been depicted in dreams as a mandala divided into four, and it seems to represent the goal of the individuation process, i.e., the self.

Following the growth of population and the increasing

dichotomy of the marriage classes, which led to a further extension of the exogamous order, all barriers gradually broke down and nothing remained but the incest-taboo. The original social order made way for other organizing factors culminating in the modern idea of the State. Now, everything that is past sinks in time into the unconscious, and this is true also of the original social order. It represented an archetype that combined exogamy and endogamy in the most fortunate way, for while it prevented marriage between brother and sister it provided a substitute in the cross-cousin marriage. This relationship is still close enough to satisfy the endogamous tendency more or less, but distant enough to include other groups and to extend the orderly cohesion of the tribe. But with the gradual abolition of exogamous barriers through increasing dichotomy, the endogamous tendency was bound to gain strength in order to give due weight to consanguineous relationships and so hold them together. This reaction was chiefly felt in the religious and then in the political field, with the growth on the one hand of religious societies and sects—we have only to think of the brotherhoods and the Christian ideal of "brotherly love"—and of nations on the other. Increasing internationalism and the weakening of religion have largely abolished or bridged over these last remaining barriers and will do so still more in the future, only to create an amorphous mass whose preliminary symptoms can already be seen in the modern phenomenon of the mass psyche. Consequently the original exogamous order is rapidly approaching a condition of chaos painfully held in check. For this there is but one remedy: the inner consolidation of the individual, who is otherwise threatened with inevitable stultification and dissolution in the mass psyche. The recent past has given us the clearest possible demonstration of what this would mean. No religion has afforded any protection, and our organizing factor, the State, has proved to be the most efficient machine for turning out mass-men. In these circumstances the immunizing of the individual against the toxin of the mass psyche is the only thing that can help. As I have already said, it is just conceivable that the endogamous tendency will intervene compensatorily and restore the consanguineous marriage, or the union of the divided components of the personality, on the psychic level—that is to say, *within* the individual. This would form a counterbalance to the progressive dichotomy and psychic dissociation of collective man.

It is of supreme importance that this process should take place *consciously*, otherwise the psychic consequences of mass-mindedness will harden and become permanent. For, if the inner consolidation of the individual is not a conscious achievement, it will occur spontaneously and will then take the well-known form of that incredible hard-heartedness which collective man displays towards his fellow men. He become a soulless herd animal governed only by panic and lust: his soul, which can live only in and from human relationships, is irretrievably lost. But the conscious achievement of inner unity clings to human relationships as to an indispensable condition, for without the conscious acknowledgment and acceptance of our fellowship with those around us there can be no synthesis of personality. That mysterious something in which the inner union takes place is nothing personal, has nothing to do with the ego, is in fact superior to the ego because, as the self, it is the synthesis of the ego and the supra-personal unconscious. The inner consolidation of the individual is not just the hardness of collective man on a higher plane, in the form of spiritual aloofness and inaccessibility: it emphatically includes our fellow man.

To the extent that the transference is projection and nothing more, it divides quite as much as it connects. But experience teaches that there is one connection in the transference which does not break off with the severance of the projection. That is because there is an extremely important instinctive factor behind it: the kinship libido. This has been pushed so far into the background by the unlimited expansion of the exogamous tendency that it can find an outlet, and a modest one at that, only within the immediate family circle, and sometimes not even there, because of the quite justifiable resistance to incest. While exogamy was limited by endogamy, it resulted in a natural organization of society which has entirely disappeared today. Everyone is now a stranger among strangers. Kinship libido—which could still engender a satisfying feeling of belonging together, as for instance in the early Christian communities—has long been deprived of its object. But, being an instinct, it is not to be satisfied by any mere substitute such as a creed, party, nation, or state. It wants the *human* connection. That is the core of the whole transference phenomenon, and it is impossible to argue it away, because relationship to the self is at once relationship to our fellow man, and no one can be related to the latter until he is related to himself.

If the transference remains at the level of projection, the connection it establishes shows a tendency to regressive concretization, i.e., to an atavistic restoration of the primitive social order. This tendency has no possible foothold in our modern world, so that every step in this direction only leads to a deeper conflict and ultimately to a real transference neurosis. Analysis of the transference is therefore an absolute necessity, because the projected contents must be reintegrated if the patient is to gain the broader view he needs for free decision.

If, however, the projection is broken, the connection—whether it be negative (hate) or positive (love)—may collapse for the time being so that nothing seems to be left but the politeness of a professional tête-à-tête. One cannot begrudge either doctor or patient a sigh of relief when this happens, although one knows full well that the problem has only been postponed for both of them. Sooner or later, here or in some other place, it will present itself again, for behind it there stands the restless urge towards individuation.

Individuation has two principal aspects: in the first place it is an internal and subjective process of integration, and in the second it is an equally indispensable process of objective relationship. Neither can exist without the other, although sometimes the one and sometimes the other predominates. This double aspect has two corresponding dangers. The first is the danger of the patient's using the opportunities for spiritual development arising out of the analysis of the unconscious as a pretext for evading the deeper human responsibilities, and for affecting a certain "spirituality" which cannot stand up to moral criticism; the second is the danger that atavistic tendencies may gain the ascendency and drag the relationship down to a primitive level. Between this Scylla and that Charybdis there is a narrow passage, and both medieval Christian mysticism and alchemy have contributed much to its discovery.

Looked at in this light, the bond established by the transference—however hard to bear and however incomprehensible it may seem—is vitally important not only for the individual but also for society, and indeed for the moral and spiritual progress of mankind. So, when the psychotherapist has to struggle with difficult transference problems, he can at least take comfort in these reflections. He is not just working for this particular patient, who may be quite insignificant, but for himself as well and his own soul, and in so doing he is perhaps laying an infinitesimal grain in the scales of humanity's soul. Small and invisible as this contribution may be, it is yet an *opus magnum*, for it is accomplished in a sphere but lately visited by the numen, where the whole weight of mankind's problems has settled. The ultimate questions of psychotherapy are not a private matter—they represent a supreme responsibility.

3

THE NAKED TRUTH

The text to this picture (Fig. 3) is, with a few alterations, a quotation from the "Tractatus aureus." [1] It runs: "He who would be initiated into this art and secret wisdom must put away the vice of arrogance, must be devout, righteous, deep-witted, humane towards his fellows, of a cheerful countenance and a happy disposition, and respectful withal. Likewise he must be an observer of the eternal secrets that are revealed to him. My son, above all I admonish thee to fear God who seeth what manner of man thou art [*in quo dispositionis tuae visus est*] and in whom is help for the solitary, whosoever he may be [*adiuvatio cuiuslibet sequestrati*]." [2] And the *Rosarium* adds from Pseudo-Aristotle: "Could God but find a man of faithful understanding, he would open his secret to him." [3]

This appeal to obviously moral qualities makes one thing quite clear: the *opus* demands not only intellectual and technical ability as in the study and practice of modern chemistry; it is a moral as well as a psychological undertaking. The texts are full of such admonitions, and they indicate the kind of attitude that is required in the execution of a religious work. The alchemists undoubtedly understood the *opus* in this sense, though it is difficult to square our picture with such an exordium. The chaste disguises have fallen away. [4] Man and woman confront one another in unabashed naturalness. Sol says, "O Luna, let [5] me be thy husband," and Luna, "O Sol, I must submit to thee." The dove bears the inscription: "Spir-

[1] An Arabic treatise whose origin is still obscure. It is printed in *Ars chemica*, and (with scholia) in *Bibl. chem. curiosa*, I, pp. 400ff.
[2] This passage is rather different in the original text (*Ars chemica*, p. 14): "in quo est nisus tuae dispositionis, et adunatio cuiuslibet sequestrati." Cf. *Psychology and Alchemy*, par. 385 and n. 87.
[3] *Art. aurif.*, II, pp. 227–28.
[4] Cf. Cant. 5 :3: "I have put off my garment."
[5] Original is illegible: ?vgan.

PHILOSOPHORVM.

seipsis secundum equalitatē inspiſsentur. Solus
enim calor tēperatus eſt humiditatis inspiſsatiuus
et mixtionis perfectiuus, et non super excedens.
Nā generatiões et procreationes rerū naturaliū
habent solū fieri per tēperatiſsimū calorē et equa
lē, vti eſt solus fimus equinus humidus et calidus.

D

Figure 3

itus est qui unificat." [6] This remark hardly fits the unvarnished
eroticism of the picture, for if what Sol and Luna say—who,
be it noted, are brother and sister—means anything at all, it
must surely mean earthly love. But since the spirit descending
from above is stated to be the mediator,[7] the situation acquires
another aspect: it is supposed to be a union in the spirit. This
is borne out admirably by one important detail in the picture: the contact of left hands has ceased. Instead, Luna's left
hand and Sol's right hand now hold the branches (from which
spring the *flores Mercurii,* corresponding to the three pipes of
the fountain), while Luna's right and Sol's left hand are touch-
ing the flowers. The left-handed relationship is no more: the
two hands of both are now connected with the "uniting symbol." This too has been changed: there are only three flowers
instead of five, it is no longer an ogdoad but a hexad,[8] a six-
rayed figure. The double quaternity has thus been replaced by
a double triad. This simplification is evidently the result of the
fact that two elements have each paired off, presumably with
their opposites, for according to alchemical theory each element
contains its opposite "within" it. Affinity, in the form of a "lov-

---

[6] This is the reading of the 1593 edition. The first edition of 1550 has "vivificat."

[7] The dove is also the attribute of the goddess of love and was a symbol of *amor coniugalis* in ancient times.

[8] Cf. Joannes Lydus, *De mensibus,* II, 11: "The sixth day they ascribe to Phos-
phorus [morning star], who is the begetter of warmth and generative moisture
[γονίμως ὑγραίνοντι]. Perhaps this is the son of Aphrodite, like Hesperus the
evening star, as appeared to the Greeks. Aphrodite we could call the nature of the
visible universe, the first-born Hyle which the oracle names star-like ['Ἀστερίαν] as
well as heavenly. The number 6 is most skilled in begetting [γεννητικώτατος], for
it is even and uneven, partaking both of the active nature on account of the
uneven [περιττὸν also means "superfluous" or "excessive"], and of the hylical
nature on account of the even, for which reason the ancients also named it marriage and harmony. For among those that follow the number 1, it is the only
number perfect in all its parts, being composed of these: its halves of the number
3, its thirds of the number 2, and its sixths of the number 1 [6 = 3 + 2 + 1].
And they say also that it is both male and female, like Aphrodite herself, who is
of male and female nature and is accordingly called hermaphroditic by the theologians. And another says that the number 6 is soul-producing [or belongs
to the ψυχογονία, ψυχογονικός], because it multiplies itself into the world-
sphere [ἐπιπεδούμενος = πολλαπλασιασμός], and because in it the opposites are
mingled. It leads to like-mindedness [ὁμόνοιαν] and friendship, giving health to
the body, harmony to songs and music, virtue to the soul, prosperity to the state,
and forethought [πρόνοιαν] to the universe."

ing" approach, has already achieved a partial union of the elements, so that now only one pair of opposites remains: masculine-feminine or *agens-patiens,* as indicated by the inscription. In accordance with the axiom of Maria, the elementary quaternity has become the active triad, and this will lead to the *coniunctio* of the two.

Psychologically we can say that the situation has thrown off the conventional husk and developed into a stark encounter with reality, with no false veils or adornments of any kind. Man stands forth as he really is and shows what was hidden under the mask of conventional adaptation: the shadow. This is now raised to consciousness and integrated with the ego, which means a move in the direction of wholeness. Wholeness is not so much perfection as completeness. Assimilation of the shadow gives a man body, so to speak; the animal sphere of instinct, as well as the primitive or archaic psyche, emerge into the zone of consciousness and can no longer be repressed by fictions and illusions. In this way man becomes for himself the difficult problem he really is. He must always remain conscious of the fact that he is such a problem if he wants to develop at all. Repression leads to a one-sided development if not to stagnation, and eventually to neurotic dissociation. Today it is no longer a question of "How can I get rid of my shadow?"—for we have seen enough of the curse of one-sidedness. Rather we must ask ourselves: "How can man live with his shadow without its precipitating a succession of disasters?" Recognition of the shadow is reason enough for humility, for genuine fear of the abysmal depths in man. This caution is most expedient, since the man without a shadow thinks himself harmless precisely because he is ignorant of his shadow. The man who recognizes his shadow knows very well that he is not harmless, for it brings the archaic psyche, the whole world of the archetypes, into direct contact with the conscious mind and saturates it with archaic influences. This naturally adds to the dangers of "affinity," with its deceptive projections and its urge to assimilate the object in terms of the projection, to draw it into the family circle in order to actualize the hidden incest situation, which seems all the more attractive and fascinating the less it is understood. The advantage of the situation, despite all its dangers, is that once the naked truth has been revealed the discussion can get down to essentials; ego and shadow are no longer divided but are brought together in an—admittedly precarious—unity. This is a great step forward, but at the same time it shows up the "differentness" of one's partner all the more clearly, and the unconscious usually tries to close the gap by increasing the attraction, so as to bring about the desired union somehow or other. All this is borne out by the alchemical idea that the fire which maintains the process must be temperate to begin with and must then gradually be raised to the highest intensity.

4

IMMERSION IN THE BATH

A new motif appears in this picture: the bath. In a sense this takes us back to the first picture of the Mercurial Fountain, which represents the "upwelling." The liquid is Mercurius, not only of the three but of the "thousand" names. He stands for the mysterious psychic substance which nowadays we would call the unconscious psyche. The rising fountain of the unconscious has reached the king and queen, or rather they have descended into it as into a bath. This is a theme with many variations in alchemy. Here are a few of them: the king is in danger of drowning in the sea; he is a prisoner under the sea; the sun drowns in the mercurial fountain; the king sweats in the glass-house; the green lion swallows the sun; Gabricus disappears into the body of his sister Beya, where he is dissolved into atoms; and so forth. Interpreted on the one hand as a harmless bath and on the other hand as the perilous encroachment of the "sea," the earth-spirit Mercurius in his watery form now begins to attack the royal pair from *below,* just as he had previously descended from above in the shape of the dove. The contact of left hands in Figure 2 has evidently roused the spirit of the deep and called up a rush of water.

The immersion in the "sea" signifies the *solutio*—"dissolution" in the physical sense of the word and at the same time, according to Dorn, the solution of a problem.[1] It is a return to the dark initial state, to the amniotic fluid of the gravid uterus. The alchemists frequently point out that their stone grows like a child in its mother's womb; they call the *vas*

---

[1] Dorn, "Speculativae philosophiae," p. 303: "Studio philosophorum comparatur putrefactio chemica. . . . Ut per solutionem corpora solvuntur, ita per cognitionem resolvuntur philosophorum dubia" (The chemical putrefaction can be compared with the study of the philosophers. . . . As bodies are dissolved through the *solutio,* so the doubts of the philosophers are resolved through knowledge).

hermeticum the uterus and its contents the foetus. What is said of the *lapis* is also said of the water: "This stinking water contains everything it needs."[2] It is sufficient unto itself, like the Uroboros, the tail-eater, which is said to beget, kill, and devour itself. *Aqua est, quae occidit et vivificat*—the water is that which kills and vivifies.[3] It is the *aqua benedicta*, the lustral water,[4] wherein the birth of the new being is prepared. As the text to our picture explains: "Our stone is to be extracted from the nature of the two bodies." It also likens the water to the *ventus* of the "Tabula smaragdina," where we read: "Portavit eum ventus in ventre suo" (The wind hath carried it in his belly). The *Rosarium* adds: "It is clear that wind is air, and air is life, and life is soul, that is, oil and water."[5] The curious idea that the soul (i.e., the breath-soul) is oil and water derives from the dual nature of Mercurius. The *aqua permanens* is one of his many synonyms, and the terms *oleum, oleaginitas, unctuosum, unctuositas,* all refer to the arcane substance which is likewise Mercurius. The idea is a graphic reminder of the ecclesiastical use of various unguents and of the consecrated water. The two bodies mentioned above are represented by the king and queen, a possible reference to the *commixtio* of the two substances in the chalice of the Mass. A similar *coniunctio* is shown in the "Grandes heures du duc de Berry,"[6] where a naked "little man and woman" are being anointed by two saintly servitors in the baptismal bath of the chalice. There can be no doubt of the connections between the alchemical *opus* and the Mass, as the treatise of Melchior Cibinensis[7] proves. Our text says: "Anima est Sol et Luna." The alchemist thought in strictly

[2] Instead of the meaningless "aqua foetum" I read "aqua foetida" (*Rosarium*, p. 241). Cf. "Cons. coniug.," *Ars chemica*, p. 64: "Leo viridis, id est . . . aqua foetida, quae est mater omnium ex qua et per quam et cum qua praeparant. . . ." (The green lion, that is . . . the stinking water, which is the mother of all things, and out of it and through it and with it, they prepare . . .).

[3] *Rosarium*, p. 214. Cf. *Aurora consurgens*, I, Ch. XII, where the bride says of herself in God's words (Deut. 32 : 39): "I will kill and I will make to live . . . and there is none that can deliver out of my hand."

[4] *Rosarium*, p. 213.

[5] Ibid., p. 237. This goes back to Senior, *De chemia*, pp. 19, 31, 33.

[6] Cf. *Psychology and Alchemy*, fig. 159.

[7] "Addam et processum," *Theatr. chem.*, III, pp. 853ff. Cf. *Psychology and Alchemy*, pars. 480ff.

ROSARIVM

corrūpitur, neq̃ ex imperfecto penitus secundũ artem aliquid fieri potest. Ratio est quia ars primas dispositiones inducere non potest, sed lapis noster est res media inter perfecta & imperfecta corpora, & quod natura ipsa incepit hoc per artem ad perfectionē deducitur. Si in ipso Mercurio operari inceperis vbi natura reliquit imperfectum, inuenies in eo perfectionē et gaudebis.

Perfectum non alteratur, sed corrumpitur. Sed imperfectum bene alteratur, ergo corruptio vnius est generatio alterius.

Speculum

Figure 4

medieval trichotomous terms: [8] anything alive—and his *lapis* is undoubtedly alive—consists of corpus, anima, and spiritus. The *Rosarium* remarks (p. 239) that "the body is Venus and feminine, the spirit is Mercurius and masculine"; hence the anima, as the "vinculum," the link between body and spirit, would be hermaphroditic,[9] i.e., a *coniunctio Solis et Lunae*. Mercurius is the hermaphrodite par excellence. From all this it may be gathered that the queen stands for the body [10] and the king for the spirit,[11] but that both are unrelated without the soul, since this is the *vinculum* which holds them together.[12] If no bond of love exists, they have no soul. In our pictures the bond is effected by the dove from above and by the water from below. These constitute the link—in other words, they are the soul. Thus the underlying idea of the psyche proves it to be a half bodily, half spiritual substance, an *anima media natura*,[13] as the alchemists call it,[14] an hermaphroditic being [15] capable of uniting the opposites, but who is never complete in the individual unless related to another individual. The unrelated human being lacks wholeness, for he can achieve wholeness only through the soul, and the soul cannot exist without its other side, which is always found in a "You." Wholeness is a combi-

---

[8] *Aurora consurgens*, I, Ch. IX, "qualis pater talis filius, talis et Spiritus Sanctus et hi tres unum sunt, corpus, spiritus et anima, quia omnis perfectio in numero ternario consistit, hoc est mensura, numero et pondere" (Like as the Father is, so is the Son, and so also is the Holy Spirit, and these three are One, body, spirit, and soul, for all perfection consisteth in the number three, that is, in measure, number, and weight.)

[9] "Anima vocatur Rebis." "Exercitationes in Turbam," *Art. aurif.*, I, p. 180.

[10] According to Firmicus Maternus (*Mathesis* V, pref., ed. Kroll and Skutsch, II, p. 3), Luna is "humanorum corporum mater."

[11] Psychologically one should read *mens* for *spiritus*.

[12] Sometimes the spirit is the *vinculum*, or else the latter is a *natura ignea* (Flamel, "Opusculum," *Theatr. chem.*, I, p. 887).

[13] Cf. "De arte chimica," *Art. aurif.*, I, pp. 584ff., and Mylius, *Phil. ref.*, p. 9.

[14] Cf. "Turba," *Art. aurif.*, I, p. 180: ". . . Spiritus et corpus unum sunt mediante anima, quae est apud spiritum et corpus. Quod si anima non esset, tunc spiritus et corpus separarentur ab invicem per ignem, sed anima adiuncta spiritui et corpori, hoc totum non curat ignem nec ullam rem mundi." (. . . The spirit and the body are one, the soul acting as a mediator which abides with the spirit and the body. If there were no soul, the spirit and the body would be separated from each other by the fire, but because the soul is joined to the spirit and the body, this whole is unaffected by fire or by any other thing in the world.)

[15] Cf. Winthuis, *Das Zweigeschlechterwesen*.

nation of I and You, and these show themselves to be parts of a transcendent unity [16] whose nature can only be grasped symbolically, as in the symbols of the *rotundum,* the rose, the wheel,[17] or the *coniunctio Solis et Lunae.* The alchemists even go so far as to say that the *corpus, anima,* and *spiritus* of the arcane substance are one, "because they are all from the One, and of the One, and with the One, which is the root of itself" (Quia ipsa omnia sunt ex uno et de uno et cum uno, quod est radix ipsius).[18] A thing which is the cause and origin of itself can only be God, unless we adopt the implied dualism of the Paracelsists, who were of the opinion that the *prima materia* is an *increatum.*[19] Similarly, the pre-Paracelsist *Rosarium* [20] maintains that the quintessence is a "self-subsistent body, differing from all the elements and from everything composed thereof."

Coming now to the psychology of the picture, it is clearly a descent into the unconscious. The immersion in the bath is another "night sea journey," [21] as the "Visio Arislei" proves. There the philosophers are shut up with the brother-sister pair in a triple glass-house at the bottom of the sea by the *Rex Marinus.* Just as, in the primitive myths, it is so stiflingly hot in the belly of the whale that the hero loses his hair, so the philosophers suffer very much from the intense heat [22] during their confinement. The hero-myths deal with rebirth and apocatastasis, and the "Visio" likewise tells of the resuscitation of the dead Thabritius (Gabricus) or, in another version, of his rebirth.[23] The night sea journey is a kind of *descensus ad in-*

[16] I do not, of course, mean the synthesis or identification of two individuals, but the conscious union of the ego with everything that has been projected into the "You." Hence wholeness is the product of an intrapsychic process which depends essentially on the relation of one individual to another. Relationship paves the way for individuation and makes it possible, but is itself no proof of wholeness. The projection upon the feminine partner contains the anima and sometimes the self.

[17] Cf. *Psychology and Alchemy,* index.   [18] *Rosarium,* p. 369.

[19] *Psychology and Alchemy,* pars. 430ff.   [20] P. 251.

[21] Cf. Frobenius, *Das Zeitalter des Sonnengottes.*

[22] "Visio Arislei," *Art. aurif.,* I, p. 148: "Mansimus in tenebris undarum et intenso aestatis calore ac maris perturbatione" (We remained in the darkness of the waves and in the intense heat of summer and the perturbation of the sea).

[23] Cf. the birth of Mithras "from the sole heat of libido" (de solo aestu libidinis." Jerome, *Adversus Jovinianum* (Migne, *P.L.,* vol. 23, col. 246). In Arabic alchemy, too, the fire that causes the fusion is called "libido." Cf. "Exercitationes in Turbam."

feros—a descent into Hades and a journey to the land of ghosts somewhere beyond this world, beyond consciousness, hence an immersion in the unconscious. In our picture the immersion is effected by the rising up of the fiery, chthonic Mercurius, presumably the sexual libido which engulfs the pair [24] and is the obvious counterpart to the heavenly dove. The latter has always been regarded as a love-bird, but it also has a purely spiritual significance in the Christian tradition accepted by the alchemists. Thus the pair are united *above* by the symbol of the Holy Ghost, and it looks as if the immersion in the bath were also uniting them *below*, i.e., in the water which is the counterpart of spirit ("It is death for souls to become water," says Heraclitus). Opposition and identity at once—a philosophical problem only when taken as a psychological one!

This development recapitulates the story of how the Original Man (Nous) bent down from heaven to earth and was wrapped in the embrace of Physis—a primordial image that runs through the whole of alchemy. The modern equivalent of this stage is the conscious realization of sexual fantasies which colour the transference accordingly. It is significant that even in this quite unmistakable situation the pair are still holding on with both hands to the starry symbol brought by the Holy Ghost, which signalizes the meaning of their relationship: man's longing for transcendent wholeness.

Art. aurif., I, p. 181: "Inter supradicta tria (scil., corpus, anima, spiritus) inest libido," etc. (Between the aforementioned three, i.e., body, soul, spirit, there is a libido).

[24] See the inscription to fig. 5a:

> "But here King Sol is tight shut in,
> And *Mercurius philosophorum* pours over him."

The sun drowning in the mercurial fountain (*Rosarium*, p. 315) and the lion swallowing the sun (p. 367) both have this meaning, which is also an allusion to the *ignea natura* of Mercurius (Leo is the House of the Sun). For this aspect of Mercurius see "The Spirit Mercurius," Part II, sec. 3.

5

THE CONJUNCTION

O Luna, folded in my sweet embrace /
Be you as strong as I, as fair of face.
O Sol, brightest of all lights known to men /
And yet you need me, as the cock the hen.
[*Figure 5*]

The sea has closed over the king and queen, and they have
gone back to the chaotic beginnings, the *massa confusa*. Physis
has wrapped the "man of light" in a passionate embrace. As the
text says: "Then Beya [the maternal sea] rose up over Gabricus
and enclosed him in her womb, so that nothing more of him was
to be seen. And she embraced Gabricus with so much love that
she absorbed him completely into her own nature, and dissolved
him into atoms." These verses from Merculinus are then quoted:

Candida mulier, si rubeo sit nupta marito,
Mox complexantur, complexaque copulantur,
Per se solvuntur, per se quoque conficiuntur,
Ut duo qui fuerant, unum quasi corpore fiant.

(White-skinned lady, lovingly joined to her ruddy-limbed husband,
Wrapped in each other's arms in the bliss of connubial union,
Merge and dissolve as they come to the goal of perfection:
They that were two are made one, as though of one body.)

In the fertile imagination of the alchemists, the hierosgamos of Sol and Luna continues right down to the animal kingdom, as is shown by the following instructions: "Take a Coetanean dog and an Armenian bitch, mate them, and they
will bear you a son in the likeness of a dog." [1] The symbolism
is about as crass as it could be. On the other hand the *Rosarium* [2]

---

[1] *Rosarium*, p. 248. Quotation from Kalid, "Liber secretorum alchemiae," *Art.
aurif.*, I, p. 340. [Cf. par. 353, n. 1.—EDITORS.]
[2] P. 247.

says: "In hora coniunctionis maxima apparent miracula" (In the hour of conjunction the greatest marvels appear). For this is the moment when the *filius philosophorum* or *lapis* is begotten. A quotation from Alfidius [3] adds: "Lux moderna ab eis gignitur" (The new light is begotten by them). Kalid says of the "son in the likeness of a dog" that he is "of a celestial hue" and that "this son will guard you . . . in this world and in the next." [4] Likewise Senior: "She hath borne a son who served his parents in all things, save that he is more splendid and refulgent than they," [5] i.e., he outshines the sun and moon. The real meaning of the *coniunctio* is that it brings to birth something that is one and united. It restores the vanished "man of light" who is identical with the Logos in Gnostic and Christian symbolism and who was there before the creation; we also meet him at the beginning of the Gospel of St. John. Consequently we are dealing with a cosmic idea, and this amply explains the alchemists' use of superlatives.

The psychology of this central symbol is not at all simple. On a superficial view it looks as if natural instinct had triumphed. But if we examine it more closely we note that the coitus is taking place in the water, the *mare tenebrositatis,* i.e., the unconscious. This idea is borne out by a variant of the picture (Figure 5a). There again Sol and Luna are in the water, but both are winged. They thus represent spirit—they are aerial beings, creatures of thought. The texts indicate that Sol and Luna are two *vapores* or *fumi* which gradually develop as the fire

[3] P. 248.

[4] Kalid, "Liber secretorum alchemiae," *Art. aurif.,* I, p. 340: "Et dixit Hermes patri suo: Pater timeo ab inimico in mea mansione. Et dixit: Fili, accipe canem masculum Corascencm et caniculam Armeniae et iunge in simul et parient canem coloris coeli et imbibe ipsum una siti ex aqua maris: quia ipse custodiet tuum amicum et custodiet te ab inimico tuo et adiuvabit te ubicumque sis, semper tecum existendo in hoc mundo et in alio." (And Hermes said to his father: Father, I am afraid of the enemy in my house. And he said: My son, take a Corascene dog and an Armenian bitch, join them together, and they will beget a dog of a celestial hue, and if ever he is thirsty, give him sea water to drink: for he will guard your friend, and he will guard you from your enemy, and he will help you wherever you may be, always being with you, in this world and in the next.)

[5] *Rosarium,* p. 248. The radiant quality ($\sigma\tau i\lambda\beta\omega\nu$) is characteristic of Mercurius and also of the first man, Gayomart or Adam. Cf. Christensen, *Les Types du premier homme,* pp. 22ff., and Kohut, "Die talmudisch-midraschische Adamssage," pp. 68, 72, 87.

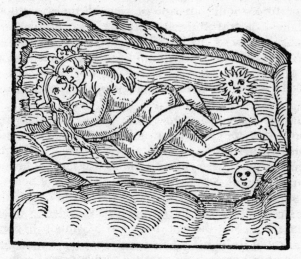

O Luna durch meyn vmbgeben/vnd suſſe mynne/
Wirſtu ſchön/ſtarck/vnd gewaltig als ich byn·

O Sol/ du biſt vber alle liecht zu erkennen/
So bedarffſtu doch mein als der han der hennen·

ARISLEVS IN VISIONE.

Coniunge ergo filium tuum Gabricum dile-
ctiorem tibi in omnibus filijs tuis cum sua sorore
Beya

Figure 5

increases in heat, and which then rise as on wings from the *decoctio* and *digestio* of the *prima materia*.[6] That is why the paired opposites are sometimes represented as two birds fighting[7] or as winged and wingless dragons.[8] The fact that two aerial creatures should mate on or beneath the water does not disturb the alchemist in the least, for he is so familiar with the changeable nature of his synonyms that for him water is not only fire but all sorts of astonishing things besides. If we interpret the water as steam we may be getting nearer the truth. It refers to the boiling solution in which the two substances unite.

As to the frank eroticism of the pictures, I must remind the reader that they were drawn for medieval eyes and that consequently they have a symbolical rather than a pornographic meaning. Medieval hermeneutics and meditation could contemplate even the most delicate passages in the Song of Songs without taking offence and view them through a veil of spirituality. Our pictures of the *coniunctio* are to be understood in this sense: union on the biological level is a symbol of the *unio oppositorum* at its highest. This means that the union of opposites in the royal art is just as real as coitus in the common acceptation of the word, so that the *opus* becomes an analogy of the natural process by means of which instinctive energy is transformed, at least in part, into symbolical activity. The creation of such analogies frees instinct and the biological sphere as a whole from the pressure of unconscious contents. Absence of symbolism, however, overloads the sphere of instinct.[9] The analogy contained in Figure 5 is a little too obvious for our modern taste, so that it almost fails in its purpose.

---

[6] The "Practica Mariae" (*Art. aurif.*, I, p. 321) makes the two into four: "[Kibrich et Zubech] . . . ipsa sunt duo fumi complectentes duo lumina" (They are the two vapours enveloping the two lights). These four evidently correspond to the four elements, since we read on p. 320: ". . . si sunt apud homines omnia 4 elementa, dixit compleri possent et complexionari et coagulari eorum fumi. . . ." (If there are in men all 4 elements, he says, their vapours could be completed and commingled and coagulated).

[7] See Lambspringk, "Figurae," *Musaeum hermeticum.*

[8] Title-page to Colonna, *Le Songe de Poliphile.* See *Psychology and Alchemy*, fig. 4.

[9] Hence the ambivalent saying in Mylius, *Phil. ref.*, p. 182: "In habentibus symbolum facilis est transitus" (For those who have the symbol the passage is easy).

FERMENTATIO.

Hye wird Sol aber verschlossen
Vnd mit Mercurio philosophorum ybergossen.

Figure 5a

As every specialist knows, the psychological parallels encountered in medical practice often take the form of fantasy-images which, when drawn, differ hardly at all from our pictures. The reader may remember the typical case I mentioned earlier (par. 377ff.), where the act of conception was represented symbolically and, exactly nine months later, the unconscious, as though influenced by a *suggestion à échéance,* produced the symbolism of a birth, or of a new-born child, without the patient's being conscious of the preceding psychic conception or having consciously reckoned the period of her "pregnancy." As a rule the whole process passes off in a series of dreams and is discovered only retrospectively, when the dream material comes to be analysed. Many alchemists compute the duration of the *opus* to be that of a pregnancy, and they liken the entire procedure to such a period of gestation.[10]

The main emphasis falls on the *unio mystica,* as is shown quite clearly by the presence of the uniting symbol in the earlier pictures. It is perhaps not without deeper significance that this symbol has disappeared in the pictures of the *coniunctio.* For at this juncture the meaning of the symbol is fulfilled: the partners have themselves become symbolic. At first each represented two elements; then each of them united into one (integration of the shadow); and finally the two together with the third become a whole—"ut duo qui fuerant, unum quasi corpore fiant." Thus the axiom of Maria is fulfilled. In this union the Holy Ghost disappears as well, but to make up for that, Sol and Luna themselves become spirit. The real meaning, therefore, is Goethe's "higher copulation," [11] a union in unconscious identity, which could be compared with the primitive, initial state of chaos, the *massa confusa,* or rather with the state of *participation mystique* where heterogeneous factors merge in an unconscious relationship. The *coniunctio* differs from this not as a mechanism but because it is by nature never an initial state: it is always the product of a process or the goal of endeavour. This is equally the case in psychology, though

10 Cf. Kalid, "Liber trium verborum," *Art aurif.,* I, pp. 355f.

    11 "No more shall you stay a prisoner
       Wrapped in darkest obfuscation;
       New desires call you upwards
       To the higher copulation."—*West-östlicher Divan.*

here the *coniunctio* comes about unintentionally and is opposed to the bitter end by all biologically minded and conscientious doctors. That is why they speak of "resolving the transference." The detachment of the patient's projections from the doctor is desirable for both parties and, if successful, may be counted as a positive result. This is a practical possibility when, owing to the patient's immaturity, or his disposition, or because of some misunderstanding arising out of the projection, or because reason and plain common sense demand it, the continued transformation of projected unconscious contents comes to a hopeless standstill, and at the same time an opportunity presents itself from outside for the projection to be switched to another object. This solution has about the same merit as persuading a person not to go into a monastery or not to set out on a dangerous expedition or not to make a marriage which everybody agrees would be stupid. We cannot rate reason highly enough, but there are times when we must ask ourselves: do we really know enough about the destinies of individuals to enable us to give good advice under *all* circumstances? Certainly we must act according to our best convictions, but are we so sure that our convictions are for the best as regards the other person? Very often we do not know what is best for ourselves, and in later years we may come to thank God from the bottom of our hearts that his kindly hand preserved us from the "reasonableness" of our former plans. It is easy for the critic to say after the event, "Ah, but that wasn't the right sort of reason!" Who can know with unassailable certainty when he has the right sort? Moreover, is it not essential to the true art of living, sometimes, in defiance of all reason and fitness, to include the unreasonable and the unfitting within the ambiance of the possible?

It should therefore not surprise us to find that there are not a few cases where, despite every effort, no possibility presents itself of resolving the transference, although the patient is—from the rational point of view—equipped with the necessary understanding and neither he nor the doctor can be accused of any technical negligence or oversight. Both of them may be so deeply impressed by the vast irrationality of the unconscious as to come to the conclusion that the best thing is to cut the Gordian knot with a drastic decision. But the surgical partition of these Siamese twins is a perilous operation.

There may be successes, though in my experience they are few and far between. I am all for a conservative solution of the problem. If the situation really is such that no other possibilities of any kind can be considered, and the unconscious obviously insists on the retention of the tie, then the treatment must be continued hopefully. It may be that the severance will only occur at a later stage, but it may also be a case of psychological "pregnancy" whose natural outcome must be awaited with patience, or again it may be one of those fatalities which, rightly or wrongly, we take on our own shoulders or else try to avoid. The doctor knows that always, wherever he turns, man is dogged by his fate. Even the simplest illness may develop surprising complications; or, equally unexpectedly, a condition that seemed very serious may take a turn for the better. Sometimes the doctor's art helps, sometimes it is useless. In the domain of psychology especially, where we still know so little, we often stumble upon the unforeseen, the inexplicable—something of which we can make neither head nor tail. Things cannot be forced, and wherever force seems to succeed it is generally regretted afterwards. Better always to be mindful of the limitations of one's knowledge and ability. Above all one needs forbearance and patience, for often time can do more than art. Not everything can and must be cured. Sometimes dark moral problems or inexplicable twists of fate lie hidden under the cloak of a neurosis. One patient suffered for years from depressions and had an unaccountable phobia about Paris. She managed to rid herself of the depressions, but the phobia proved inaccessible. However, she felt so well that she was prepared to risk ignoring her phobia. She succeeded in getting to Paris, and the next day she lost her life in a car smash. Another patient had a peculiar and abiding horror of flights of steps. One day he got caught up in some street-rioting and shots were fired. He found himself in front of a public building with a broad flight of steps leading up to it. In spite of his phobia he dashed up them to seek shelter inside the building, and fell on the steps, mortally wounded by a stray bullet.

These examples show that psychic symptoms need to be judged with the greatest caution. This is also true of the various forms of transference and its contents. They sometimes set the doctor almost insoluble problems or cause him all manner worries which may go to the limits of the endurable and even beyond. Particularly if he has a marked ethical personality and takes his psychological work seriously, this may lead to moral conflicts and divided loyalties whose real or supposed incompatibility has been the occasion of more than one disaster. On the basis of long experience I would therefore like to warn against too much therapeutic enthusiasm. Psychological work is full of snags, but it is just here that incompetents swarm. The medical faculties are largely to blame for this, because for years they refused to admit the psyche among the aetiological factors of pathology, even though they had no other use for it. Ignorance is certainly never a recommendation, but often the best knowledge is not enough either. Therefore I say to the psychotherapist: let no day pass without humbly remembering that everything has still to be learned.

The reader should not imagine that the psychologist is in any position to explain what "higher copulation" is, or the *coniunctio,* or "psychic pregnancy," let alone the "soul's child." Nor should one feel annoyed if the newcomer to this delicate subject, or one's own cynical self, gets disgusted with these—as he thinks them—phoney ideas and brushes them aside with a pitying smile and an offensive display of tact. The unprejudiced scientific inquirer who seeks the truth and nothing but the truth must guard against rash judgments and interpretations, for here he is confronted with *psychological facts* which the intellect cannot falsify and conjure out of existence. There are among one's patients intelligent and discerning persons who are just as capable as the doctor of giving the most disparaging interpretations, but who cannot avail themselves of such a weapon in the face of these insistent facts. Words like "nonsense" only succeed in banishing little things—not the things that thrust themselves tyrannically upon you in the stillness and loneliness of the night. The images welling up from the unconscious do precisely that. What we choose to call this fact does not affect the issue in any way. If it is an illness, then this *morbus sacer* must be treated according to its nature. The doctor can solace himself with the reflection that he, like the rest of his colleagues, does not only have patients who are curable, but chronic ones as well, where curing becomes nursing. At all events the empirical material gives us no sufficient grounds for always talking about "illness"; on the contrary, one comes to realize that it is a moral problem and often one wishes for a priest who, instead of confessing and proselytizing, would just listen, obey, and put this singular matter before God so that He could decide.

Patientia et mora are absolutely necessary in this kind of work. One must be able to wait on events. Of work there is plenty—the careful analysis of dreams and other unconscious contents. Where the doctor fails, the patient will fail too, which is why the doctor should possess a real knowledge of these things and not just opinions, the offscourings of our modern philosophy for everyman. In order to augment this much-needed knowledge, I have carried my researches back to those earlier times when naïve introspection and projection were still at work, mirroring a psychic hinterland that is virtually blocked for us today. In this way I have learned much for my own practice, especially as regards understanding the formidable fascination of the contents in question. These may not always strike the patient as particularly fascinating, so he suffers instead from a proportionately strong compulsive tie in whose intensity he can rediscover the force of those subliminal images. He will, however, try to interpret the tie rationalistically in the spirit of the age, and consequently does not perceive and will not admit the irrational foundations of his transference, namely the archetypal images.

6

DEATH

Here King and Queen are lying dead/
In great distress the soul is sped.
[*Figure 6*]

Vas hermeticum, fountain, and sea have here become sarcophagus and tomb. King and queen are dead and have melted
into a single being with two heads. The feast of life is followed
by the funereal threnody. Just as Gabricus dies after becoming
united with his sister, and the son-lover always comes to an early
end after consummating the hierosgamos with the mother-
goddess of the Near East, so, after the *coniunctio oppositorum,*
deathlike stillness reigns. When the opposites unite, all energy
ceases: there is no more flow. The waterfall has plunged to its
full depth in that torrent of nuptial joy and longing; now only
a stagnant pool remains, without wave or current. So at least it
appears, looked at from the outside. As the legend tells us, the
picture represents the *putrefactio,* the corruption, the decay of a
once living creature. Yet the picture is also entitled "Concep-
tio." The text says: "Corruptio unius generatio est alterius"—
the corruption of one is the generation of the other,[1] an indication that this death is an interim stage to be followed by a new
life. No new life can arise, says the alchemists, without the death
of the old. They liken the art to the work of the sower, who
buries the grain in the earth: it dies only to waken to new life.[2]

---

[1] "Tractatulus Avicennae," *Art. aurif.,* I, p. 426.

[2] Cf. *Aurora,* I, Ch. XII (after John 12:24). Hortulanus (Ruska, *Tabula,* p. 186):
"Vocatur [lapis] etiam granum frumenti, quod nisi mortuum fuerit, ipsum solum
manet," etc. (It [the stone] is also called the grain of wheat, which remains itself
alone, unless it dies). Equally unhappy is the other comparison, also a favourite:
"Habemus exemplum in ovo quod putrescit primo, et tunc gignitur pullus, qui
post totum corruptum est animal vivens" (We have an example in the egg: first
it putrefies and then the chick is born, a living animal sprung from the corruption of the whole).—*Rosarium,* p. 255.

Thus with their *mortificatio, interfectio, putrefactio, combustio, incineratio, calcinatio,* etc., they are imitating the work of nature. Similarly they liken their labours to human mortality, without which the new and eternal life cannot be attained.[3]

The corpse left over from the feast is already a new body, a *hermaphroditus* (a compound of Hermes-Mercurius and Aphrodite-Venus). For this reason one half of the body in the alchemical illustrations is masculine, the other half feminine (in the *Rosarium* this is the left half). Since the *hermaphroditus* turns out to be the long-sought *rebis* or *lapis,* it symbolizes that mysterious being yet to be begotten, for whose sake the *opus* is undertaken. But the *opus* has not yet reached its goal, because the *lapis* has not come alive. The latter is thought of as animal, a living being with body, soul, and spirit. The legend says that the pair who together represented body and spirit are dead, and that the soul (evidently only *one*[4] soul) parts from them "in great distress."[5] Although various other meanings play a part here, one cannot rid oneself of the impression that the death is a sort of tacit punishment for the sin of incest, for "the wages of sin is death."[6] That would explain the soul's "great distress" and also the blackness mentioned in the variant of our picture[7] ("Here is Sol turned black").[8] This blackness is

[3] Cf. Ruska, *Turba,* p. 139: "Tunc autem, doctrinae filii, illa res igne indiget, quousque illius corporis spiritus vertatur et per noctes dimittatur, ut homo in suo tumulo, et pulvis fiat. His peractis reddet ei Deus et animam suam et spiritum, ac infirmitate ablata confortatur illa res . . . quemadmodum homo post resurrectionem fortior fit," etc. (But, sons of the doctrine, that thing will need fire, until the spirit of its body is changed and is sent away through the nights, like a man in his grave, and becomes dust. When this has happened, God will give back to it its soul and its spirit and, with all infirmity removed, that thing is strengthened . . . as a man becomes stronger after the resurrection.)

[4] Cf. the ψυχογονία in Lydus' account of the hexad, supra, par. 451, n. 8.

[5] Cf. Senior, *De chemia,* p. 16: ". . . et reviviscit, quod fuerat morti deditum, post inopiam magnam" (What had been given over to death, comes to life again after great tribulation).

[6] For the alchemist, this had a precedent in Gen. 2 : 17: "for in the day that thou eatest thereof thou shalt surely die." Adam's sin is part of the drama of the creation. "Cum peccavit Adam, eius est anima mortua" (When Adam sinned his soul died), says Gregory the Great (Epist. CXIV, Migne, *P.L.,* vol. 77, col. 806).

[7] *Art. aurif.,* II, p. 324.

[8] The *nigredo* appears here not as the initial state but as the product of a prior process. The time-sequence of phases in the *opus* is very uncertain. We see the same uncertainty in the individuation process, so that a typical sequence of stages

PHILOSOPHORVM.
CONCEPTIO SEV PVTRE
factio

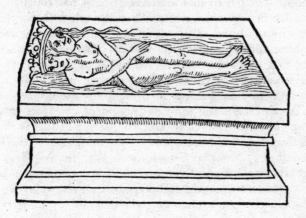

Hye ligen könig vnd köningin dot/
Die sele scheydt sich mit grosser not.

ARISTOTELES REX ET
Philosophus.

Nunquam vidi aliquod animatum crescere sine putrefactione, nisi autem fiat putridum inuanum erit opus alchimicum.

Figure 6

the *immunditia* (uncleanliness), as is proved by the *ablutio* that subsequently becomes necessary. The *coniunctio* was incestuous and therefore sinful, leaving pollution behind it. The *nigredo* always appears in conjunction with *tenebrositas*, the darkness of the tomb and of Hades, not to say of Hell. Thus the descent that began in the marriage-bath has touched rock bottom: death, darkness, and sin. For the adept, however, the hopeful side of things is shown in the anticipated appearance of the hermaphrodite, though the psychological meaning of this is at first obscure.

The situation described in our picture is a kind of Ash Wednesday. The reckoning is presented, and a dark abyss yawns. Death means the total extinction of consciousness and the complete stagnation of psychic life, so far as this is capable of consciousness. So catastrophic a consummation, which has been the object of annual lamentations in so many places (e.g. the laments for Linus, Tammuz,[9] and Adonis), must surely correspond to an important archetype, since even today we have our Good Friday. An archetype always stands for some typical event. As we have seen, there is in the *coniunctio* a union of two figures, one representing the daytime principle, i.e., lucid consciousness, the other a nocturnal light, the unconscious. Because the latter cannot be seen directly, it is always projected; for, unlike the shadow, it does not belong to the ego but is collective. For this reason it is felt to be something alien to us, and we suspect it of belonging to the particular person with whom we have emotional ties. In addition a man's unconscious has a feminine character; it hides in the feminine side of him which he naturally does not see in himself but in the woman who fascinates him. That is probably why the soul (anima) is feminine. If, therefore, man and woman are merged in some kind of unconscious identity, he will take over the traits of her ani-

---

can only be constructed in very general terms. The deeper reason for this "disorder" is probably the "timeless" quality of the unconscious, where conscious succession becomes simultaneity, a phenomenon I have called "synchronicity." [Cf. Jung, "Synchronicity: An Acausal Connecting Principle."] From another point of view we would be justified in speaking of the "elasticity of unconscious time" on the analogy of the equally real "elasticity of space." For the relations between psychology and atomic physics, see Meier, "Moderne Physik."

[9] Ezek. 8 : 14: ". . . behold, there sat women weeping for Tammuz."

mus and she the traits of his anima. Although neither anima nor animus can be constellated without the intervention of the conscious personality, this does not mean that the resultant situation is nothing but a personal relationship and a personal entanglement. The personal side of it is a fact, but not the main fact. The main fact is the *subjective experience* of the situation—in other words, it is a mistake to believe that one's personal dealings with one's partner play the most important part. Quite the reverse: the most important part falls to the man's dealings with the anima and the woman's dealings with the animus. Nor does the *coniunctio* take place with the personal partner; it is a royal game played out between the active, masculine side of the woman (the animus) and the passive, feminine side of the man (the anima). Although the two figures are always tempting the ego to identify itself with them, a real understanding even on the personal level is possible only if the identification is refused. Non-identification demands considerable moral effort. Moreover it is only legitimate when not used as a pretext for avoiding the necessary degree of personal understanding. On the other hand, if we approach this task with psychological views that are too personalistic, we fail to do justice to the fact that we are dealing with an archetype which is anything but personal. It is, on the contrary, an *a priori* so universal in scope and incidence that it often seems advisable to speak less of *my* anima or *my* animus and more of *the* anima and *the* animus. As archetypes, these figures are semi-collective and impersonal quantities, so that when we identify ourselves with them and fondly imagine that we are then most truly ourselves, we are in fact most estranged from ourselves and most like the average type of *Homo sapiens*. The personal protagonists in the royal game should constantly bear in mind that at bottom it represents the "trans-subjective" union of archetypal figures, and it should never be forgotten that it is a *symbolical* relationship whose goal is complete individuation. In our series of pictures this idea is suggested *sub rosa*. Hence, when the *opus* interposes itself in the form of the rose or wheel, the unconscious and purely personal relationship becomes a psychological problem which, while it prevents a descent into complete darkness, does not in any way cancel out the operative force of the archetype. The right way, like the wrong way, must be paid for, and however much the alchemist may extol *venerabilis natura,* it is in either case an *opus contra naturam.* It goes against nature to commit incest, and it goes against nature not to yield to an ardent desire. And yet it is nature that prompts such an attitude in us, because of the kinship libido. So it is as Pseudo-Democritus says: "Nature rejoices in nature, nature conquers nature, nature rules over nature." [10] Man's instincts are not all harmoniously arranged, they are perpetually jostling each other out of the way. The ancients were optimistic enough to see this struggle not as a chaotic muddle but as aspiring to some higher order.

Thus the encounter with anima and animus means conflict and brings us up against the hard dilemma in which nature herself has placed us. Whichever course one takes, nature will be mortified and must suffer, even to the death; for the merely natural man must die in part during his own lifetime. The Christian symbol of the crucifix is therefore a prototype and an "eternal" truth. There are medieval pictures showing how Christ is nailed to the Cross by his own virtues. Other people meet the same fate at the hands of their vices. Nobody who finds himself on the road to wholeness can escape that characteristic suspension which is the meaning of crucifixion. For he will infallibly run into things that thwart and "cross" him: first, the thing he has no wish to be (the shadow); second, the thing he is not (the "other," the individual reality of the "You"); and third, his psychic non-ego (the collective unconscious). This being at cross purposes with ourselves is suggested by the crossed branches held by the king and queen, who are themselves man's cross in the form of the anima and woman's cross in the form of the animus. The meeting with the collective unconscious is a fatality of which the natural man has no inkling until it overtakes him. As Faust says: "You are conscious only of the single urge/ O may you never know the other!"

This process underlies the whole *opus,* but to begin with it is so confusing that the alchemist tries to depict the conflict, death, and rebirth figuratively, on a higher plane, first—in his *practica*—in the form of chemical transformations and then—in his *theoria*—in the form of conceptual images. The same

[10] Berthelot, *Alch. grecs,* II, i, 3: Ἡ φύσις τῇ φύσει τέρπεται, καὶ ἡ φύσις τὴν φύσιν νικᾷ καὶ ἡ φύσις τὴν φύσιν κρατεῖ.

process may also be conjectured to underlie certain religious *opera*, since notable parallels exist between ecclesiastical symbolism and alchemy. In psychotherapy and in the psychology of neuroses it is recognized as the psychic process par excellence, because it typifies the content of the transference neurosis. The supreme aim of the *opus psychologicum* is conscious realization, and the first step is to make oneself conscious of contents that have hitherto been projected. This endeavour gradually leads to knowledge of one's partner and to self-knowledge, and so to the distinction between what one really is and what is projected into one, or what one imagines oneself to be. Meanwhile, one is so taken up with one's own efforts that one is hardly conscious of the extent to which "nature" acts not only as a driving-force but as a helper—in other words, how much instinct insists that the higher level of consciousness be attained. This urge to a higher and more comprehensive consciousness fosters civilization and culture, but must fall short of the goal unless man voluntarily places himself in its service. The alchemists are of the opinion that the *artifex* is the servant of the work, and that not he but nature brings the work to fruition. All the same, there must be will as well as ability on man's part, for unless both are present the urge remains at the level of merely natural symbolism and produces nothing but a perversion of the instinct for wholeness which, if it is to fulfil its purpose, needs all parts of the whole, including those that are projected into a "You." Instinct seeks them there, in order to re-create that royal pair which every human being has in his wholeness, i.e., that bisexual First Man who has "no need of anything but himself." Whenever this drive for wholeness appears, it begins by disguising itself under the symbolism of incest, for, unless he seeks it in himself, a man's nearest feminine counterpart is to be found in his mother, sister, or daughter.

With the integration of projections—which the merely natural man in his unbounded naïveté can never recognize as such—the personality becomes so vastly enlarged that the normal ego-personality is almost extinguished. In other words, if the individual identifies himself with the contents awaiting integration, a positive or negative inflation results. Positive inflation comes very near to a more or less conscious megalomania; negative inflation is felt as an annihilation of the ego.

The two conditions may alternate. At all events the integration of contents that were always unconscious and projected involves a serious lesion of the ego. Alchemy expresses this through the symbols of death, mutilation, or poisoning, or through the curious idea of dropsy, which in the "Aenigma Merlini"[11] is represented as the king's desire to drink inordinate quantities of water. He drinks so much that he melts away and has to be cured by the Alexandrian physicians.[12] He suffers from a surfeit of the unconscious and becomes dissociated—"ut mihi videtur omnia membra mea ab invicem dividuntur" (so that all my limbs seem divided one from another).[13] As a matter of fact, even Mother Alchemia is dropsical in her lower limbs.[14] In alchemy, inflation evidently develops into a psychic oedema.[15]

The alchemists assert that death is at once the conception of the *filius philosophorum*, a peculiar variation of the doctrine of the Anthropos.[16] Procreation through incest is a royal or divine prerogative whose advantages the ordinary man is forbidden to enjoy. The ordinary man is the natural man, but the king or hero is the "supernatural" man, the *pneumatikos* who is "baptized with spirit and water," i.e., begotten in the *aqua*

[11] Merlinus probably has as little to do with Merlin the magician as "King Artus" with King Arthur. It is more likely that Merlinus is "Merculinus," a diminutive form of Mercurius and the pseudonym of some Hermetic philosopher. "Artus" is the Hellenistic name for Horus. The form "Merqûlius" and "Marqûlius" for Mercurius is substantiated in Arabic sources. Jûnân ben Marqûlius is the Greek Ion, who according to Byzantine mythology is a son of Mercurius (Chwolsohn, *Die Ssabier*, I, p. 796). Al-Maqrîzi says: "The Merqûlians . . . are the Edessenes who were in the neighbourhood of Harran," obviously the Sabaeans (ibid., II, p. 615). The Ion in Zosimos (Berthelot, *Alch. grecs*, III, i, 2) probably corresponds to the above Ion. [Cf. "The Visions of Zosimos," par. 86, n. 4.—EDITORS.]

[12] Merlinus, "Allegoria de arcano lapidis," *Art. aurif.*, I, pp. 392ff.: "Rex autem . . . bibit et rebibit, donec omnia membra sua repleta sunt, et omnes venae eius inflatae" (But the king drinks and drinks again until all his limbs are full and all his veins inflated). [Cf. *Mysterium Coniunctionis*, par. 357.—EDITORS.]

[13] In the "Tractatus aureus" (*Mus. herm.*, p. 51) the king drinks the "aqua pernigra," here described as "pretiosa et sana," for strength and health. He represents the new birth, the self, which has assimilated the "black water," i.e., the unconscious. In the Apocalypse of Baruch the black water signifies the sin of Adam, the coming of the Messiah, and the end of the world.

[14] *Aurora*, II, in *Art. aurif.*, I, p. 196.

[15] Hence the warning: "Cave ab hydropisi et diluvio Noe" (Beware of dropsy and the flood of Noah).—Ripley, *Omnia opera chemica*, p. 69.

[16] Cf. *Psychology and Alchemy*, pars. 456f.

benedicta and born from it. He is the Gnostic Christ who descends upon the man Jesus during his baptism and departs from him again before the end. This "son" is the new man, the product of the union of king and queen—though here he is not born of the queen, but queen and king are themselves transformed into the new birth.[17]

Translated into the language of psychology, the mythologem runs as follows: the union of the conscious mind or ego-personality with the unconscious personified as anima produces a new personality compounded of both—"ut duo qui fuerant, unum quasi corpore fiant." Not that the new personality is a third thing midway between conscious and unconscious, it is both together. Since it transcends consciousness it can no longer be called "ego" but must be given the name of "self." Reference must be made here to the Indian idea of the atman, whose personal and cosmic modes of being form an exact parallel to the psychological idea of the self and the *filius philosophorum*.[18] The self too is both ego and non-ego, subjective and objective, individual and collective. It is the "uniting symbol" which epitomizes the total union of opposites.[19] As such and in accordance with its paradoxical nature, it can only be expressed by means of symbols. These appear in dreams and spontaneous fantasies and find visual expression in the mandalas that occur in the patient's dreams, drawings, and paintings. Hence, properly understood, the self is not a doctrine or theory but an image born of nature's own workings, a natural symbol far removed from all conscious intention. I must stress this obvious fact because certain critics still believe that the manifestations of the unconscious can be written off as pure speculation. But they are matters of observed fact, as every doctor knows who has to deal with such cases. The integration of the self is a fundamental problem which arises in the second half of life. Dream symbols having all the characteristics of mandalas may occur long beforehand without the development of the inner man becoming an immediate problem. Isolated incidents of this kind can easily be overlooked, so that it then seems as if the phenomena I have described were rare curiosities. They

17 One of several versions.
18 This is meant only as a psychological and not as a metaphysical parallel.
19 Cf. *Psychological Types* (1923 edn., pp. 320f.).

are in fact nothing of the sort; they occur whenever the individuation process becomes the object of conscious scrutiny, or where, as in the psychoses, the collective unconscious peoples the conscious mind with archetypal figures.

7

THE ASCENT OF THE SOUL

Here is the division of the four elements/
As from the lifeless corpse the soul ascends.
[*Figure 7*]

This picture carries the *putrefactio* a stage further. Out of the decay the soul mounts up to heaven. Only *one* soul departs from the two, for the two have indeed become one. This brings out the nature of the soul as a *vinculum* or *ligamentum:* it is a function of relationship. As in real death, the soul departs from the body and returns to its heavenly source. The One born of the two represents the metamorphosis of both, though it is not yet fully developed and is still a "conception" only. Yet, contrary to the usual meaning of conception, the soul does not come down to animate the body, but leaves the body and mounts heavenwards. The "soul" evidently represents the *idea* of unity which has still to become a concrete fact and is at present only a potentiality. The idea of a wholeness made up of *sponsus* and *sponsa* has its correlate in the *rotundus globus coelestis.*[1]

This picture corresponds psychologically to a dark state of disorientation. The decomposition of the elements indicates dissociation and the collapse of the existing ego-consciousness. It is closely analogous to the schizophrenic state, and it should be taken very seriously because this is the moment when latent psychoses may become acute, i.e., when the patient becomes aware of the collective unconscious and the psychic non-ego. This collapse and disorientation of consciousness may last a considerable time and it is one of the most difficult transitions the analyst has to deal with, demanding the greatest patience, courage, and faith on the part of both doctor and patient. It is

[1] "Tractatus aureus," *Mus. herm.,* p. 47.

a sign that the patient is being driven along willy-nilly without any sense of direction, that, in the truest sense of the word, he is in an utterly *soulless* condition, exposed to the full force of autoerotic affects and fantasies. Referring to this state of deadly darkness, one alchemist says: "Hoc est ergo magnum signum, in cuius investigatione nonnulli perierunt" (This is a great sign, in the investigation of which not a few have perished).[2]

This critical state, when the conscious mind is liable to be submerged at any moment in the unconscious, is akin to the "loss of soul" that frequently attacks primitives. It is a sudden *abaissement du niveau mental,* a slackening of the conscious tension, to which primitive man is especially prone because his consciousness is still relatively weak and means a considerable effort for him. Hence his lack of will-power, his inability to concentrate and the fact that, mentally, he tires so easily, as I have experienced to my cost during palavers. The wide-spread practice of yoga and dhyana in the East is a similar *abaissement* deliberately induced for the purpose of relaxation, a technique for releasing the soul. With certain patients, I have even been able to establish the existence of subjectively experienced levitations in moments of extreme derangement.[3] Lying in bed, the patients felt that they were floating horizontally in the air a few feet above their bodies. This is a suggestive reminder of the phenomenon called the "witch's trance," and also of the parapsychic levitations reported of many saints.

The corpse in our picture is the residue of the past and represents the man who is no more, who is destined to decay. The "torments" which form part of the alchemist's procedure belong to this stage of the *iterum mori*—the reiterated death. They consist in "membra secare, arctius sequestrare ac partes mortificare et in naturam, quae in eo [lapide] est, vertere" (cutting up the limbs, dividing them into smaller and smaller pieces, mortifying the parts, and changing them into the nature which is in [the stone]), as the *Rosarium* says, quoting from Hermes. The passage continues: "You must guard the water and fire dwelling in the arcane substance and contain those waters with the permanent water, even though this be no water,

[2] Quotation from a source unknown to me, given as "Sorin" in *Rosarium*, p. 264.
[3] One such case is described in Meier, "Spontanmanifestationen," p. 290.

Hye teylen sich die vier element/
Aus dem leyb scheydt sich die sele behendt.

De

Figure 7

but the fiery form of the true water." [4] For the precious substance, the soul, is in danger of escaping from the bubbling solution in which the elements are decomposed. This precious substance is a paradoxical composite of fire and water, i.e., Mercurius, the *servus* or *cervus fugitivus* who is ever about to flee— or who, in other words, resists integration (into consciousness). He has to be "contained" by the "water," whose paradoxical nature corresponds to the nature of Mercurius and actually contains him within itself. Here we seem to have a hint about the treatment required: faced with the disorientation of the patient, the doctor must hold fast to his own orientation; that is, he must know what the patient's condition means, he must understand what is of value in the dreams, and do so moreover with the help of that *aqua doctrinae* which alone is appropriate to the nature of the unconscious. In other words, he must approach his task with views and ideas capable of grasping unconscious symbolism. Intellectual or supposedly scientific theories are not adequate to the nature of the unconscious, because they make use of a terminology which has not the slightest affinity with its pregnant symbolism. The waters must be drawn together and held fast by the one water, by the *forma ignea verae aquae*. The kind of approach that makes this possible must therefore be plastic and symbolical, and itself the outcome of personal experience with unconscious contents. It should not stray too far in the direction of abstract intellectualism; hence we are best advised to remain within the framework of traditional mythology, which has already proved comprehensive enough for all practical purposes. This does not preclude the satisfaction of theoretical requirements, but these should be reserved for the private use of the doctor.

Therapy aims at strengthening the conscious mind, and whenever possible I try to rouse the patient to mental activity and get him to subdue the *massa confusa* of his mind with his own understanding,[5] so that he can reach a vantage-point *au-*

---

[4] *Art. aurif.*, II, p. 264: "Et eorum aquas sua aqua continere, si qua non est aqua, forma ignea verae aquae."

[5] Remembering the rule that every proposition in psychology may be reversed with advantage, I would point out that it is always a bad thing to accentuate the conscious attitude when this has shown itself to be so strong in the first place as violently to suppress the unconscious.

dessus de la mêlée. Nobody who ever had any wits is in danger of losing them in the process, though there are people who never knew till then what their wits are for. In such a situation, understanding acts like a life-saver. It integrates the unconscious, and gradually there comes into being a higher point of view where both conscious and unconscious are represented. It then proves that the invasion by the unconscious was rather like the flooding of the Nile: it increases the fertility of the land. The panegyric addressed by the *Rosarium* to this state is to be taken in that sense: "O natura benedicta et benedicta est tua operatio, quia de imperfecto facis perfectum cum vera putrefactione quae est nigra et obscura. Postea facis germinare novas res et diversas, cum tua viriditate facis diversos colores apparere." (O blessed Nature, blessed are thy works, for that thou makest the imperfect to be perfect through the true putrefaction, which is dark and black. Afterwards thou makest new and multitudinous things to grow, causing with thy verdure the many colours to appear.) [6] It is not immediately apparent why this dark state deserves special praise, since the *nigredo* is universally held to be of a sombre and melancholy humour reminiscent of death and the grave. But the fact that medieval alchemy had connections with the mysticism of the age, or rather was itself a form of mysticism, allows us to adduce as a parallel to the *nigredo* the writings of St. John of the Cross [7] concerning the "dark night." This author conceives the "spiritual night" of the soul as a supremely positive state, in which the invisible—and therefore dark—radiance of God comes to pierce and purify the soul.

The appearance of the colours in the alchemical vessel, the so-called *cauda pavonis*, denotes the spring, the renewal of life—*post tenebras lux.* The text continues: "This blackness is called earth." The Mercurius in whom the sun drowns is an earth-spirit, a *Deus terrenus*,[8] as the alchemists say, or the *Sapi-*

---

[6] *Art. aurif.*, II, p. 265.

[7] *The Dark Night of the Soul.*

[8] Ventura, "De ratione conficiendi lapidis," *Theatr. chem.*, II, p. 260. There is in the gold a "quiddam essentiale Divinum" (something of Divine essence) ("Tractatus Aristotelis," *Theatr. chem.*, V, p. 892). "Natura est vis quaedam insita rebus. . . . Deus est natura et natura Deus, a Deo oritur aliquid proximum ei" (Nature is a certain force innate in things. . . . God is Nature and Nature is

entia Dei which took on body and substance in the creature by creating it. The unconscious is the spirit of chthonic nature and contains the archetypal images of the *Sapientia Dei*. But the intellect of modern civilized man has strayed too far in the world of consciousness, so that it received a violent shock when it suddenly beheld the face of its mother, the earth.

The fact that the soul is depicted as a homunculus in our picture indicates that it is on the way to becoming the *filius regius*, the undivided and hermaphroditic First Man, the Anthropos. Originally he fell into the clutches of Physis, but now he rises again, freed from the prison of the mortal body. He is caught up in a kind of ascension, and, according to the *Tabula smaragdina*, unites himself with the "upper powers." He is the essence of the "lower power" which, like the "third filiation" in the doctrine of Basilides, is ever striving upwards from the depths,[9] not with the intention of staying in heaven, but solely in order to reappear on earth as a healing force, as an agent of immortality and perfection, as a mediator and saviour. The connection with the Christian idea of the Second Coming is unmistakable.

The psychological interpretation of this process leads into regions of inner experience which defy our powers of scientific description, however unprejudiced or even ruthless we may be. At this point, unpalatable as it is to the scientific temperament, the idea of mystery forces itself upon the mind of the inquirer, not as a cloak for ignorance but as an admission of his inability to translate what he knows into the everyday speech of the intellect. I must therefore content myself with a bare mention of the archetype which is inwardly experienced at this stage, namely the birth of the "divine child" or—in the language of the mystics—the inner man.[10]

God, and from God originates something very near to him).—Penotus, "Quinquaginta septem canones," *Theatr. chem.*, II, p. 153. God is known in the *linea in se reducta* of the gold (Maier, *De circulo physico quadrato*, p. 16).

[9] Hippolytus, *Elenchos*, VII, 26, 10.

[10] Angelus Silesius, *Cherubinischer Wandersmann*, Book IV, p. 194: "The work that God loves best and most wants done/ Is this: that in you he can bear his son." Book II, p. 103: "There where God bends on you his spirit mild/ Is born within the everlasting child."

8

PURIFICATION

Here falls the heavenly dew, to lave/
The soiled black body in the grave.
[*Figure 8*]

The falling dew is a portent of the divine birth now at hand. *Ros Gedeonis* (Gideon's dew) [1] is a synonym for the *aqua permanens,* hence for Mercurius.[2] A quotation from Senior at this point in the *Rosarium* text says: "Maria says again: 'But the water I have spoken of is a king descending from heaven, and the earth's humidity absorbs it, and the water of heaven is retained with the water of the earth, and the water of the earth honours that water with its lowliness and its sand, and water consorts with water and water will hold fast to water and Albira is whitened with Astuna.' "[3]

The whitening (*albedo* or *dealbatio*) is likened to the *ortus solis,* the sunrise; it is the light, the illumination, that follows the darkness. Hermes says: "Azoth et ignis latonem abluunt et nigredinem ab eo auferunt" (Azoth and fire cleanse the lato and remove the blackness).[4] The spirit Mercurius descends in his heavenly form as *sapientia* and as the fire of the

---

[1] Cf. Judges 6 : 36ff.

[2] Cf. "The Spirit Mercurius," II, sec. 2.

[3] *Art. aurif.,* II, pp. 275f. Cf. Senior, *De chemia,* pp. 17–18: "Dixit iterum Maria: Aqua, quam iam memoravi, est rex de coelo descendens et terra cum humore suo suscepit eum et retinetur aqua coeli cum aqua terrae propter servitium suum et propter arenam suam honorat eam et congregatur aqua in aquam, Alkia in Alkiam et dealbatur Alkia cum Astuam." In the Arabic text "Astua" appears also as "Alkia"; "al-kiyān" = "vital principle" (Stapleton, *Three Arabic Treatises,* p. 152). "Alkia" occurs in the "Liber Platonis quartorum" (p. 152) in the sense of "vital principle" or "libido."

[4] Azoth is the arcane substance (cf. Senior, *De chemia,* p. 95) and the lato is the black substance, a mixture of copper, cadmium, and orichalcum (ἐλατρόν; see Du Cange, *Glossarium*).

111

Holy Ghost, to purify the blackness. Our text continues: "Deal-bate latonem et libros rumpite, ne corda vestra rumpantur.[5] Haec est enim compositio omnium Sapientum et etiam tertia pars totius operis.[6] Jungite ergo, ut dicitur in Turba, siccum humido: id est terram nigram cum aqua sua et coquite donec dealbatur. Sic habes aquam et terram per se et terram cum aqua dealbatam: illa albedo dicitur aer." (Whiten the lato and rend the books lest your hearts be rent asunder.[5] For this is the synthesis of the wise and the third part of the whole *opus*.[6] Join therefore, as is said in the *Turba*,[7] the dry to the moist, the black earth with its water, and cook till it whitens. In this man-ner you will have the essence of water and earth, having whit-ened the earth with water: but that whiteness is called air.) So that the reader may know that the "water" is the *aqua sapi-entiae,* and the dew falling from heaven the divine gift of il-lumination and wisdom, there follows a long disquisition on Wisdom, entitled "Septimum Sapientiae Salomonis":

She it is that Solomon chose to have instead of light, and above all beauty and health; in comparison of her he compared not unto her the virtue of any precious stone. For all gold in her sight shall be esteemed as a little sand, and silver shall be counted as clay; and this is not without cause, for to gain her is better than the merchan-dise of silver and the most pure gold. And her fruit is more precious than all the riches of this world, and all the things that are desired are not to be compared with her. Length of days and health are in her right hand, and in her left hand glory and infinite riches. Her ways are beautiful operations and praiseworthy, not unsightly nor

---

[5] *Rosarium*, p. 277. This oft-repeated quotation is to be found in the treatise of Morienus ("Sermo de transmutatione metallorum," *Art. aurif.*, II, pp. 7ff.), which appears to have been translated from the Arabic by Robert of Chartres in the 12th century. Morienus attributes it to the obsolete author Elbo Interfector. It must be of very early origin, but hardly earlier than the 8th century.

[6] Reference to the "Tab. smarag.": "Itaque vocatus sum Hermes Trismegistus habens tres partes philosophiae totius mundi" (Therefore I am called Hermes Trismegistus, having the three parts of the philosophy of the whole world).

[7] A classic of Arabic origin, put into Latin between the 11th and 12th centuries. The *Turba* quotation in the *Rosarium* comes from "Rosinus ad Sarratantam," *Art. aurif.*, I, pp. 284f. The *Turba* (ed. Ruska, p. 158) has only: "Siccum igitur humido miscete, quae sunt terra et aqua; ac igne et aere coquite, unde spiritus et anima desiccantur" (Therefore mix the dry with the moist, which are earth and water, and cook them with fire and air, whence spirit and soul are dried out).

ABLVTIO VEL
Mundificatio

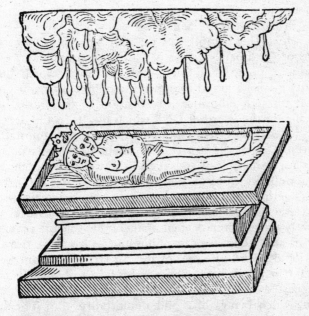

Hie felt der Tauw von himmel herab/
Vnnd wascht den schwartzen leyb im grab ab-

K iij

Figure 8

ill-favoured, and her paths are measured and not hasty,[8] but are bound up with stubborn and day-long toil. She is a tree of life to them that lay hold on her, and an unfailing light. Blessed shall they be who retain her, for the science of God shall never perish, as Alphidius beareth witness, for he saith: He who hath found this science, it shall be his rightful food for ever.[9]

In this connection I would like to point out that water as a symbol of wisdom and spirit can be traced back to the parable which Christ told to the Samaritan woman at the well.[10] The uses to which this parable was put can be seen in one of the sermons of Cardinal Nicholas of Cusa, a contemporary of our alchemists: "There is in Jacob's well a water which human ingenuity has sought and found. Philosophy is its name, and it is found through laborious investigation of the world of the senses. But in the Word of God, which dwells in the depths of the living well of Christ's humanity, there is a fountain for the refreshment of the spirit. Here, then, we have Jacob's well of the senses, the well of reason and the well of wisdom. From the first well, which is of animal nature and deep, the father drinks, together with his children and cattle; from the second, which is yet deeper and on the very margin of nature, there drink only the children of men, namely those whose reason has awakened and whom we call philosophers; from the third, the deepest of all, drink the sons of the All-Highest, whom we call gods and true theologians. Christ in his humanity may be called the deepest well. . . . In this deepest well is the source of wisdom, which brings bliss and immortality. . . . The living well bears the source of its own life, it calls the thirsty to the waters of salvation that they may be refreshed with the water

---

[8] A reference to the saying of Morienus ("De transmutatione metallorum," *Art. aurif.,* II, p. 21): ". . . omnis festinatio [scil. festinantia] ex parte Diaboli est" (. . . all haste is of the devil). Hence the *Rosarium* says (p. 352): "Ergo qui patientiam non habet ab opere manum suspendat, quia impedit cum ob festinantiam credulitas" (Therefore, he who hath not patience, let him hold back his hand from the work, for credulity will ensnare him if he hasten).

[9] *Rosarium,* p. 277. Identical with *Aurora consurgens,* I, Ch. I.

[10] John 4 : 13–14: ". . . Whosoever drinketh of this water shall thirst again: But whosoever drinketh of the water that I shall give him shall never thirst; but the water that I shall give him shall be in him a well of water springing up into everlasting life."

of saving wisdom." [11] Another passage in the same sermon says: "Whosoever drinks the spirit, drinks of a bubbling spring." [12] Finally, Cusanus says: "Mark well, our reason is given to us with the power of an intellectual seed; wherefore it contains a welling principle through which it generates in itself the water of understanding. And this well can yield naught but water of a like nature, namely, the water of human understanding; just as the understanding of the principle 'every thing either is or is not' yields the metaphysical water from which the other streams of science flow without cease." [13]

After all this there can be no more doubt that the black darkness is washed away by the *aqua sapientiae* of "our science," namely the God-given gift of the royal art and the knowledge it bestows. The *mundificatio* (purification) means, as we have seen, the removal of the superfluities that always cling to merely natural products, and especially to the symbolic unconscious contents which the alchemist found projected into matter. He therefore acted on Cardan's rule that the object of the work of interpretation is to reduce the dream material to its most general principles.[14] This is what the laboratory worker called the *extractio animae*, and what in the psychological field we

11 Koch, "Cusanus-Texte," p. 124: "In puteo Jacob est aqua, quae humano ingenio quaesita et reperta est, et potest significari quoad hoc philosophia humana, quae penetratione laboriosa sensibilium quaeritur. In Verbo autem Dei, quod est in profundo vivi putei, scl. humanitatis Christi, est fons refrigerans spiritum. Et ita notemus puteum sensibilem Jacob, puteum rationalem, et puteum sapientialem. De primo puteo, qui est naturae animalis et altus, bibit pater, filii et pecora; de secundo, qui altior in orizonte naturae, bibunt filii hominum tantum, scl. ratione vigentes, et philosophi vocantur; de tertio, qui altissimus, bibunt filii excelsi, qui dicuntur dii et sunt veri theologi. Christus secundum humanitatem puteus quidem dici potest altissimus. . . . In illo profundissimo puteo est fons sapientiae, quae praestat felicitatem et immortalitatem . . . portat vivus puteus fontem suae vitae ad sitientes, vocat sitientes ad aquas salutares, ut aqua sapientiae salutaris reficiantur."

12 Ibid., p. 132: "Qui bibit spiritum, bibit fontem scaturientem."

13 Ibid., p. 134: "Adhuc nota, quod intellectus nobis datus est cum virtute seminis intellectualis: unde in se habet principium fontale, mediante quo in seipso generat aquam intelligentiae, et fons ille non potest nisi aquam suae naturae producere, scl. humanae intelligentiae, sicut intellectus principii, 'quodlibet est vel non est' producit aquas metaphysicales, ex quibus alia flumina scientiarum emanant indesinenter."

14 Cardan, *Somniorum synesiorum:* "Unumquodque somnium ad sua generalia deducendum est."

would call the working through of the idea contained in the dream. We know that this requires a necessary premise or hypothesis, a certain intellectual structure by means of which "apperceptions" can be made. In the case of the alchemist, such a premise was ready to hand in the *aqua (doctrinae)*, or the God-inspired *sapientia* which he could also acquire through a diligent study of the "books," the alchemical classics. Hence the reference to the books, which at this stage of the work must be avoided or destroyed "lest your hearts be rent asunder." This singular exhortation, altogether inexplicable from the chemical point of view, has a profound significance here. The absolvent water or *aqua sapientiae* had been established in the teachings and sayings of the masters as the *donum Spiritus Sancti* which enables the philosopher to understand the *miracula operis*. Therefore he might easily be tempted to assume that philosophical knowledge is the highest good, as the Cusanus quotation shows. The psychological equivalent of this situation is when people imagine that they have reached the goal of the work once the unconscious contents have been made conscious and theoretically evaluated. In both cases this would be arbitrarily to define "spirit" as a mere matter of thinking and intuition. Both disciplines, it is true, are aiming at a "spiritual" goal: the alchemist undertakes to produce a new, volatile (hence aerial or "spiritual") entity endowed with *corpus, anima, et spiritus*, where *corpus* is naturally understood as a "subtle" body or "breath body"; the analyst tries to bring about a certain attitude or frame of mind, a certain "spirit" therefore. But because the body, even when conceived as the *corpus glorificationis*, is grosser than *anima* and *spiritus*, a "remnant of earth" necessarily clings to it, albeit a very subtle one.[15] Hence an at-

---

[15] ". . . subtilietur lapis, donec in ultimam subtilitatis puritatem deveniat et ultimo volatilis fiat" (The stone should be subtilized until it reaches the ultimate purity of refinement and becomes, in the end, volatile).—*Rosarium*, p. 351. Or again (ibid., p. 285): "Sublimatio est duplex: Prima est remotio superfluitatis, ut remaneant partes purissimae a faecibus elementaribus segregatae sicque virtutem quintae essentiae possideant. Et haec sublimatio est corporum in spiritum reductio cum scilicet corporalis densitas transit in spiritus subtilitatem." (Sublimation is twofold: The first is the removal of the superfluous so that the purest parts shall remain, free from elementary dregs, and shall possess the quality of the quintessence. The other sublimation is the reduction of the bodies to spirit, i.e., when the corporeal density is transformed into a spiritual subtlety.)

titude that seeks to do justice to the unconscious as well as to one's fellow human beings cannot possibly rest on knowledge alone, in so far as this consists merely of thinking and intuition. It would lack the function that perceives values, i.e., feeling, as well as the *fonction du réel,* i.e., sensation, the sensible perception of reality.[16]

Thus if books and the knowledge they impart are given exclusive value, man's emotional and affective life is bound to suffer. That is why the purely intellectual attitude must be abandoned. "Gideon's dew" is a sign of divine intervention, it is the moisture that heralds the return of the soul.

The alchemists seem to have perceived the danger that the work and its realization may get stuck in one of the conscious functions. Consequently they stress the importance of the *theoria,* i.e., intellectual understanding as opposed to the *practica,* which consisted merely of chemical experiments. We might say that the *practica* corresponds to pure perception, and that this must be supplemented by apperception. But this second stage still does not bring complete realization. What is still lacking is heart or feeling, which imparts an abiding value to anything we have understood. The books must therefore be "destroyed" lest thinking impair feeling and thus hinder the return of the soul.

These difficulties are familiar ground to the psychotherapist. It often happens that the patient is quite satisfied with merely registering a dream or fantasy, especially if he has pretensions to aestheticism. He will then fight against even intellectual understanding because it seems an affront to the reality of his psychic life. Others try to understand with their brains only, and want to skip the purely practical stage. And when they have understood, they think they have done their full share of realization. That they should also have a *feeling-relationship* to the contents of the unconscious seems strange to them or even ridiculous. Intellectual understanding and aestheticism both produce the deceptive, treacherous sense of liberation and superiority which is liable to collapse if feeling intervenes. Feeling always binds one to the reality and meaning of symbolic

[16] Cf. *Psychological Types,* Part II, Definitions 20 [*Coll. Works* edn., Def. 21], 35, 47, 53.

contents, and these in turn impose binding standards of ethical behaviour from which aestheticism and intellectualism are only too ready to emancipate themselves.

Owing to the almost complete lack of psychological differentiation in the age of alchemy, it is hardly surprising that such considerations as these are only hinted at in the treatises. But hints do exist, as we have seen. Since then the differentiation of the functions has increased apace, with the result that they have become more and more segregated from one another. Consequently it is very easy for the modern mind to get stuck in one or other of the functions and to achieve only an incomplete realization. It is hardly necessary to add that in time this leads to a neurotic dissociation. To this we owe the further differentiation of the individual functions as well as the discovery of the unconscious, but at the price of psychological disturbance. Incomplete realization explains much that is puzzling both in the individual and in the contemporary scene. It is a crucial matter for the psychotherapist, particularly for those who still believe that intellectual insight and routine understanding, or even mere recollection, are enough to effect a cure. The alchemists thought that the *opus* demanded not only laboratory work, the reading of books, meditation, and patience, but also love.

Nowadays we would speak of "feeling-values" and of realization through feeling. One is often reminded of Faust's shattering experience when he was shaken out of the "deadly dull rut" of his laboratory and philosophical work by the revelation that "feeling is all." In this we can already see the modern man who has got to the stage of building his world on a single function and is not a little proud of his achievement. The medieval philosophers would certainly never have succumbed to the idea that the demands of feeling had opened up a new world. The pernicious and pathological slogan *l'art pour l'art* would have struck them as absurd, for when they contemplated the mysteries of nature, sensation, creation, thinking, cognition and feeling were all one to them. Their state of mind was not yet split up into so many different functions that each stage of the realization process would have needed a new chapter of life. The story of Faust shows how unnatural our condition is: it required the intervention of the devil—in anticipation of Steinach [17]—to transform the ageing alchemist into a young gallant and make him forget himself for the sake of the all-too-youthful feelings he had just discovered! That is precisely the risk modern man runs: he may wake up one day to find that he has missed half his life.

Nor is realization through feeling the final stage. Although it does not really belong to this chapter, yet it might not be out of place to mention the fourth stage after the three already discussed, particularly since it has such a very pronounced symbolism in alchemy. This fourth stage is the anticipation of the *lapis*. The imaginative activity of the fourth function—intuition, without which no realization is complete—is plainly evident in this anticipation of a possibility whose fulfilment could never be the object of empirical experience at all: already in Greek alchemy it was called λίθος οὐ λίθος "the stone that is no stone." Intuition gives outlook and insight; it revels in the garden of magical possibilities as if they were real. Nothing is more charged with intuitions than the *lapis philosophorum*. This keystone rounds off the work into an experience of the totality of the individual. Such an experience is completely foreign to our age, although no previous age has ever needed wholeness so much. It is abundantly clear that this is the prime problem confronting the art of psychic healing in our day, as a consequence of which we are now trying to loosen up our rigid *psychologie à compartiments* by putting in a few communicating doors.

After the ascent of the soul, with the body left behind in the darkness of death, there now comes an enantiodromia: the *nigredo* gives way to the *albedo*. The black or unconscious state that resulted from the union of opposites reaches the nadir and a change sets in. The falling dew signals resuscitation and a new light: the ever deeper descent into the unconscious suddenly becomes illumination from above. For, when the soul vanished at death, it was not lost; in that other world it formed the living counterpole to the state of death in this world. Its reappearance from above is already indicated by the dewy moisture. This dewiness partakes of the nature of the psyche, for ψυχή is cognate with ψυχρός (cold) and ψυχόω (to freshen and animate), while on the other hand dew is synonymous with the

17 [Eugen Steinach (1861–1944), Austrian physiologist who experimented with rejuvenation by grafting animal glands.—EDITORS.]

aqua permanens, the *aqua sapientiae,* which in turn signifies illumination through the realization of meaning. The preceding union of opposites has brought light, as always, out of the darkness of night, and by this light it will be possible to see what the real meaning of that union was.

9

THE RETURN OF THE SOUL

Here is the soul descending from on high/
To quick the corpse we strove to purify.

[*Figure 9*]

Here the reconciler, the soul, dives down from heaven to
breathe life into the dead body. The two birds at the bottom
left of the picture represent the allegorical winged and wingless dragons in the form of fledged and unfledged birds.[1] This is
one of the many synonyms for the double nature of Mercurius,
who is both a chthonic and a pneumatic being. The presence
of this divided pair of opposites means that although the
hermaphrodite appears to be united and is on the point of coming alive, the conflict between them is by no means finally resolved and has not yet disappeared: it is relegated to the "left"
and to the "bottom" of the picture, i.e., banished to the sphere
of the unconscious. The fact that these still unintegrated opposites are represented theriomorphically (and not anthro-
pomorphically as before) bears out this supposition.

The text of the *Rosarium* continues with a quotation from
Morienus: "Despise not the ash, for it is the diadem of thy

[1] Cf. Lambspringk's *Symbols, Mus. Herm.*, p. 355, with the verses:

"Nidus in sylva reperitur	(A nest is found in the forest
in quo Hermes suos pullos habet,	In which Hermes has his birds.
Unus semper conatur volatum,	One always tries to fly away,
Alter in nido manere gaudet,	The other rejoices in the nest to stay
Et alter alterum non dimittit."	And will not let the other go.)

This image comes from Senior, *De chemia*, p. 15: "Abscisae sunt ab eo alae et
pennae et est manens, non recedens ad superiora" (Its wings are cut off and its
feathers, and it is stationary, not returning to the heights). Likewise Stolcius de
Stolcenberg, *Viridarium chymicum*, Fig. XXXIII. In Maier, *De circulo*, p. 127,
the opposites are represented as "vultur in cacumine montis et corvus sine alis"
(a vulture on the peak of the mountain and a raven without wings). Cf. "Tractatus aureus," *Ars chem.*, pp. 11–12, and "Rosinus ad Sarratantam," *Art. aurif.*,
I, p. 316.

heart." This ash, the inert product of incineration, refers to the dead body, and the admonition establishes a curious connection between body and heart which at that time was regarded as the real seat of the soul.[2] The diadem refers of course to the supremely kingly ornament. Coronation plays some part in alchemy—the *Rosarium,* for instance, has a picture [3] of the *Coronatio Mariae,* signifying the glorification of the white, moonlike (purified) body. The text then quotes Senior as follows: "Concerning the white tincture: When my beloved parents have tasted of life, have been nourished with pure milk and become drunk with my white substance, and have embraced each other in my bed, they shall bring forth the son of the moon, who will excel all his kindred. And when my beloved has drunk from the red rock sepulchre and tasted the maternal fount in matrimony, and has drunk with me of my red wine and lain with me in my bed in friendship, then I, loving him and receiving his seed into my cell, shall conceive and become pregnant and when my time is come shall bring forth a most mighty son, who shall rule over and govern all the kings and princes of the earth, crowned with the golden crown of victory by the supreme God who liveth and reigneth for ever and ever." [4]

The coronation picture that illustrates this text [5] proves that the resuscitation of the purified corpse is at the same time a glorification, since the process is likened to the crowning of the Virgin.[6] The allegorical language of the Church supports

2 Cf. "Paracelsus as a Spiritual Phenomenon," pars. 201f.

3 *Psychology and Alchemy,* fig. 235.

4 *Art. aurif.,* II, p. 377: "De Tinctura alba: Si parentes dilecti mei de vita gustaverint et lacte mero lactati fuerint et meo albo inebriati fuerint et in lectulo meo nupserint, generabunt filium Lunae, qui totam parentelam suam praevalebit. Et si dilectus meus de tumulo rubeo petrae potaverit et fontem matris suae gustaverit et inde copulatus fuerit et vino meo rubeo et mecum inebriatus fuerit et in lecto [meo] mihi amicabiliter concubuerit, et in amore meo sperma suum cellulam meam subintraverit, concipiam et ero praegnans et tempore meo pariam filium potentissimum, dominantem et regnantem prae cunctis regibus et principibus terrae, coronatum aurea corona victoriae, ad omnia a Deo altissimo, qui vivit et regnat in seculorum secula." Cf. "Cons. coniug.," *Ars chem.,* p. 129, and "Rosinus ad Sarratantam," pp. 291ff.

5 The style of the pictures dates them to the 16th cent., but the text may be a century older. Ruska (*Tab. smarag.,* p. 193) assigns the text to the 14th cent. The later dating, 15th cent. (Ruska, *Turba,* p. 342), is probably the more accurate.

6 *Psychology and Alchemy,* par. 500.

PHILOSOPHORVM

ANIMÆ IVBILATIO SEV
Ortus seu Sublimatio.

hie schwingt sich die sele hernidder/
Vnd erquickt den gereinigten leychnam wider.

L iij

Figure 9

such a comparison. The connections of the Mother of God with the moon,[7] water, and fountains are so well known that I need not substantiate them further. But whereas it is the Virgin who is crowned here, in the Senior text it is the son who receives the "crown of victory"—which is quite in order since he is the *filius regius* who replaces his father. In *Aurora* the crown is given to the *regina austri*, Sapientia, who says to her beloved: "I am the crown wherewith my beloved is crowned," so that the crown serves as a connection between the mother and her son-lover.[8] In a later text [9] the *aqua amara* is defined as "crowned with light." At that time Isidore of Seville's etymology was still valid: *mare ab amaro*,[10] which vouches for "sea" as synonymous with the *aqua permanens*. It is also an allusion to the water symbolism of Mary (πηγή, "fountain").[11] Again and again we note that the alchemist proceeds like the unconscious in the choice of his symbols: every idea finds both a positive and a negative expression. Sometimes he speaks of a royal pair, sometimes of dog and bitch; and the water symbolism is likewise expressed in violent contrasts. We read that the royal diadem appears "in menstruo meretricis (in the menstruum of a whore)," [12] or the following instructions are given: "Take the foul deposit [*faecem*] that remains in the cooking-vessel and preserve it, for it is the crown of the heart." The deposit corresponds to the corpse in the sarcophagus, and the sarcophagus corresponds in turn to the mercurial fountain or the *vas hermeticum*.

---

[7] See ibid., fig. 220.

[8] Cant. 3:11: ". . . see king Solomon in the diadem, wherewith his mother crowned him in the day of his espousals." Gregory the Great comments that the mother is Mary "quae coronavit eum diademate, quia humanitatem nostram ex ea ipsa assumpsit. . . . Et hoc in die desponsationis eius . . . factum esse dicitur: quia quando unigenitus filius Dei divinitatem suam humanitati nostrae copulare voluit, quando. . . . Ecclesiam sponsam suam sibi assumere placuit: tunc . . . carnem nostram ex matre Virgine suscipere voluit" (who crowned him with the crown because he assumed our human nature from her. . . . And that is said to have been done on the day of his espousals, because, when the only-begotten son of God wished to join his divinity with our human nature, he decided to take unto himself, as his bride, the Church. Then it was that he willed to assume our flesh from his virgin mother).—St Gregory, *Super Cantica Canticorum expositio*, ch. III (Migne, *P.L.*, vol. 79, col. 507.)

[9] "Gloria mundi," *Mus. herm.*, p. 213.

[10] *Liber etymologiarum*, XIII, 14.   [11] *Psychology and Alchemy*, par. 92.

[12] Philalethes, "Introitus apertus," *Mus. herm.*, p. 654.

The soul descending from heaven is identical with the dew, the *aqua divina,* which, as Senior, quoting Maria, explains, is "Rex de coelo descendens." [13] Hence this water is itself crowned and forms the "diadem of the heart," [14] in apparent contradiction to the earlier statement that the ash was the diadem. It is difficult to tell whether the alchemists were s hopelessly muddled that they did not notice these flat contradictions, or whether their paradoxes were sublimely deliberate. I suspect it was a bit of both, since the *ignorantes, stulti, fatui* would take the texts at their face value and get bogged in the welter of analogies, while the more astute reader, realizing the necessity for symbolism, would handle it like a virtuoso with no trouble at all. Intellectual responsibility seems always to have been the alchemists' weak spot, though a few of them tell us plainly enough how we are to regard their peculiar language.[15] The less respect they showed for the bowed shoulders

---

[13] *De chemia,* p. 17.

[14] It is just possible that the idea of the *diadema* is connected with the cabalistic *Kether* (corona). The *Diadema purpureum* is *Malchuth,* "the female," "the bride." Purple relates to the *vestimentum,* an attribute to the Shekinah (the Divine Presence), which "enim est Vestis et Palatium Modi Tiphereth, non enim potest fieri mentio Nominis Tetragrammati nisi in Palatio eius, quod est Adonai. Apellaturque nomine *Diadematis,* quia est Corona in capite mariti sui"(. . . is the Garment and the Palace of the Modus Tiphereth [Glory], for no mention can be made of the Four-Letter Name which is Adonai, except in His Palace. And it is called by the name of Diadem because it is the crown on the head of the husband).—Knorr von Rosenroth, *Kabbala denudata,* I, p. 131. ". . . Malchuth vocatur Kether nempe corona legis," etc. (Malchuth is called Kether since it is the crown of the Law). "Sephirah decima vocatur Corona: quia est mundus Dilectionum, quae omnia circumdant," etc. (The tenth Sephira [number] is called the crown, because it is the world of delights which surround all things).—Ibid., p. 487. "[Corona] sic vocatur Malchuth, quando ascendit usque ad Kether; ibi enim existens est Corona super caput mariti sui" [The Crown] is called Malchuth when it ascends up to Kether; for there is the crown upon the head of the husband).—Ibid., p. 624. Cf. Goodenough, "The Crown of Victory in Judaism."

[15] Norton's "Ordinall" (*Theatr. chem. britannicum,* p. 40) says:

> "For greatly doubted evermore all suche,
> That of this Scyence they may write too muche:
> Every each of them tought but one pointe or twayne,
> Whereby his fellowes were made certayne:
> How that he was to them a Brother,
> For every of them understoode each other;
> Alsoe they wrote not every man to teache,
> But to shew themselves by a secret speache:

of the sweating reader, the greater was their debt, willing or unwilling, to the unconscious, for it is just the infinite variety of their images and paradoxes that points to a psychological fact of prime importance: the indefiniteness of the archetype with its multitude of meanings, all presenting different facets of a single, simple truth. The alchemists were so steeped in their inner experiences that their sole concern was to devise fitting images and expressions regardless of whether these were intelligible or not. Although in this respect they remained behind

---

Trust not therefore to reading of one Boke,
But in many Auctors works ye may looke;
Liber librum apperit saith Arnolde the great Clerke."

"The Book of Krates" (Berthelot, *Moyen âge*, III, p. 52) says: "Your intentions are excellent, but your soul will never bring itself to divulge the truth, because of the diversities of opinion and of wretched pride." Hoghelande ("De alch. diff.," *Theatr. chem.*, I, p. 155) says: "At haec [scientia] . . . tradit opus suum immiscendo falsa veris et vera falsis, nunc diminute nimium, nunc superabundanter, et sine ordine, et saepius praepostero ordine, et nititur obscure tradere et occultare quantum potest" (This [science] transmits its work by mixing the false with the true and the true with the false, sometimes very briefly, at other times in a most prolix manner, without order and quite often in the reverse order; and it endeavours to transmit [the work] obscurely, and to hide it as much as possible). Senior (*De chemia*, p. 55) says: "Verum dixerunt per omnia, Homines vero non intelligunt verba eorum . . . unde falsificant veridicos, et verificant falsificos opinionibus suis. . . . Error enim eorum est ex ignorantia intentionis eorum, quando audiunt diversa verba, sed ignota intellectui eorum, cum sint in intellectu occulto." (They told the truth in regard to all things, but men do not understand their words . . . whence through their assumptions they falsify the verities and verify the falsities. . . . The error springs from ignorance of their [the writers'] meaning, when they hear divers words unknown to their understanding, since these have a hidden meaning.) Of the secret hidden in the words of the wise, Senior says: "Est enim illud interius subtiliter perspicientis et cognoscentis" (For this belongs to him who subtly perceives and is cognizant of the inner meaning). The *Rosarium* (p. 230) explains: "Ego non dixi omnia apparentia et necessaria in hoc opere, quia sunt aliqua quae non licet homini loqui" (So I have not declared all that appears and is necessary in this work, because there are things of which a man may not speak). Again (p. 274): "Talis materia debet tradi mystice, sicut poësis fabulose et parabolice" (Such matters must be transmitted in mystical terms, like poetry employing fables and parables). Khunrath (*Von hyl. Chaos*, p. 21) mentions the saying: "Arcana publicata vilescunt" (secrets that are published become cheap)—words which Andreae used as a motto for his *Chymical Wedding*. Abū'l Qāsim Muhammad ibn Ahmad al-Simāwī, known as al-Irāqī, says in his "Book of the Seven Climes" (see Holmyard, "Abū'l-Qāsim," p. 410) regarding Jābir ibn Hayyān's method of instruction: "Then he spoke enigmatically concerning the composition of the External

the times, they nevertheless performed the inestimable service of having constructed a phenomenology of the unconscious long before the advent of psychology. We, as heirs to these riches, do not find our heritage at all easy to enjoy. Yet we can comfort ourselves with the reflection that the old masters were equally at a loss to understand one another, or that they did so only with difficulty. Thus the author of the *Rosarium* says that the "antiqui Philosophi tam obscure quam confuse scripserunt," so that they only baffled the reader or put him off altogether. For his part, he says, he would make the "experimentum verissimum" plain for all eyes to see and reveal it "in the most certain and human manner"—and then proceeds to write exactly like all the others before him. This was inevitable, as the alchemists did not really know what they were writing about. Whether we know today seems to me not altogether sure. At any rate we no longer believe that the secret lies in chemical substances, but that it is rather to be found in one of the darker and deeper layers of the psyche, although we do not know the nature of this layer. Perhaps in another century or so we shall discover a new darkness from which there will emerge something we do not understand either, but whose presence we sense with the utmost certainty.

The alchemist saw no contradiction in comparing the diadem with a "foul deposit" and then, in the next breath, saying that it is of heavenly origin. He follows the rule laid down in the "Tabula smaragdina": "Quod est inferius, est sicut quod est superius. Et quod est superius, est sicut quod est inferius." [16] His faculty for conscious discrimination was not as acute as modern man's, and was distinctly blunter than the

---

and the Internal. . . . Then he spoke darkly . . . that in the External there is no complete tincture and that the complete tincture is to be found only in the Internal. Then he spoke darkly . . . saying, Verily we have made the External nothing more than a veil over the Internal . . . that the Internal is like this and like that and he did not cease from this kind of behaviour until he had completely confused all except the most quick-witted of his pupils. . . ." Wei Po-yang (*c.* 142 A.D.) says: "It would be a great sin on my part not to transmit the Tao which would otherwise be lost to the world forever. I shall not write on silk lest the divine secret be unwittingly spread abroad. In hesitation I sigh. . . ." ("An Ancient Chinese Treatise," p. 243).

[16] The parallel to this is the paradoxical relation of Malchuth to Kether, the lowest to the highest (see note 14 above).

scholastic thought of his contemporaries. This apparent regression cannot be explained by any mental backwardness on the part of the alchemist; it is more the case that his main interest is focussed on the unconscious itself and not at all on the powers of discrimination and formulation which mark the concise conceptual thinking of the schoolmen. He is content if he succeeds in finding expressions to delineate afresh the secret he feels. How these expressions relate to and differ from one another is of the smallest account to him, for he never supposes that anybody could reconstruct the art from his ideas about it, but that those who approach the art at all are already fascinated by its secret and are guided by sure intuition, or are actually elected and predestined thereto by God. Thus the *Rosarium* [17] says, quoting Hortulanus: [18] "Solus ille, qui scit facere lapidem Philosophorum, intelligit verba eorum de lapide" (Only he who knows how to make the philosophers' stone can understand their words concerning it). The darkness of the symbolism scatters before the eyes of the enlightened philosopher. Hortulanus says again: "Nihil enim prodest occultatio philosophorum in sermonibus, ubi doctrina Spiritus sancti operatur" [19] (The mystification in the sayings of the philosophers is of no avail where the teaching of the Holy Ghost is at work).

The alchemist's failure to distinguish between *corpus* and *spiritus* is in our case assisted by the assumption that, owing to the preceding *mortificatio* and *sublimatio,* the body has taken on "quintessential" or spiritual form and consequently, as a *corpus mundum* (pure substance), is not so very different from spirit. It may shelter spirit or even draw it down to itself.[20] All

[17] P. 270.
[18] He is thought to be identical with Joannes de Garlandia, who lived in the second half of the 12th cent. and wrote the "Commentarius in Tabulam smaragdinam," in *De alchemia* (1541).
[19] Ibid., p. 365. Since the alchemists were, as "philosophers," the empiricists of the psyche, their terminology is of secondary importance compared with their experience, as is the case with empiricism generally. The discoverer is seldom a good classifier.
[20] Thus Dorn ("Physica Trismegisti," *Theatr. chem.*, I, p. 409) says: "Spagirica foetura terrestris caelicam naturam induat per ascensum, et deinceps suo descensu centri naturam terreni recipiat" (This earthly, spagyric birth clothes itself with heavenly nature by its ascent, and then by its descent visibly puts on the nature of the centre of the earth).

these ideas lead one to conclude that not only the *coniunctio* but the reanimation of the "body" is an altogether transmundane event, a process occurring in the psychic non-ego. This would explain why the process is so easily projected, for if it were of a personal nature its liability to projection would be considerably reduced, because it could then be made conscious without too much difficulty. At any rate this liability would not have been sufficient to cause a projection upon inanimate matter, which is the polar opposite of the living psyche. Experience shows that the carrier of the projection is not just *any* object but is always one that proves adequate to the nature of the content projected—that is to say, it must offer the content a "hook" to hang on.[21]

Although the process is essentially transcendental, the projection brings it down to reality by violently affecting the conscious and personal psyche. The result is an inflation, and it then becomes clear that the *coniunctio* is a hierosgamos of the gods and not a mere love-affair between mortals. This is very subtly suggested in the *Chymical Wedding*, where Rosencreutz, the hero of the drama, is only a guest at the feast and, though forbidden to do so, slips into the bedchamber of Venus in order to gaze admiringly on the naked beauty of the sleeper. As a punishment for this intrusion Cupid wounds him in the hand with an arrow.[22] His own personal, secret connection with the royal marriage is only fleetingly indicated right at the end: the king, alluding to Rosencreutz, says that he (Rosencreutz) was his father.[23] Andreae, the author, must have been a man of some wit, since at this point he tries to extricate himself from the affair with a jest. He gives a clear hint that he himself is the father of his characters and gets the king to confirm this. The voluntarily proffered information about the paternity of this "child" is the familiar attempt of a creative artist to bolster up the prestige of his ego against the suspicion that he is the victim of the creative urge welling out of the unconscious. Goethe could not shake off the grip of *Faust*—his "main busi-

---

[21] This explains why the projection usually has some influence on the carrier, which is why the alchemists in their turn expected the "projection" of the stone to bring about a transmutation of base metals.

[22] The alchemists regarded the arrow as the *telum passionis* of Mercurius.

[23] Rosencreutz, *The Chymical Wedding*, p. 212.

ness"—half so easily. (Lesser men have correspondingly more need of greatness, hence they must make others think more highly of them.) Andreae was as fascinated by the secret of the art as any alchemist; the serious attempt he made to found the Rosicrucian Order is proof of this, and it was largely for reasons of expediency, owing to his position as a cleric, that he was led to adopt a more distant attitude in later years.[24]

If there is such a thing as an unconscious that is not personal—i.e., does not consist of individually acquired contents, whether forgotten, subliminally perceived, or repressed—then there must also be processes going on in this non-ego, spontaneous archetypal events which the conscious mind can only perceive when they are projected. They are immemorially strange and unknown, and yet we seem to have known them from everlasting; they are also the source of a remarkable fascination that dazzles and illuminates at once. They draw us like a magnet and at the same time frighten us; they manifest themselves in fantasies, dreams, hallucinations, and in certain kinds of religious ecstasy.[25] The *coniunctio* is one of these archetypes. The absorptive power of the archetype explains not only the widespread incidence of this motif but also the passionate intensity with which it seizes upon the individual, often in defiance of all reason and understanding. To the *peripeteia* of the *coniunctio* also belong the processes illustrated in the last few pictures. They deal with the after-effects of the fusion of opposites, which have involved the conscious personality in their union. The extreme consequence of this is the dissolution of the ego in the unconscious, a state resembling death. It results from the more or less complete identification of the ego with unconscious factors, or, as we would say, from contamination. This is what the alchemists experienced as *immunditia*, pollution. They saw it as the defilement of something transcendent by the gross and opaque body which had for that reason to undergo sublimation. But the body, psychologically speaking, is the expression of our individual and conscious existence, which, we then feel, is in danger of being swamped or poisoned by the unconscious. We

24 Waite, *Real History of the Rosicrucians.*
25 Intoxicants that induce delirious states can also release these processes, for which purpose datura (Jimson weed) and peyotl are used in primitive rites. See Hastings, *Encyclopedia,* IV, pp. 735f.

therefore try to separate the ego-consciousness from the unconscious and free it from that perilous embrace. Yet, although the power of the unconscious is feared as something sinister, this feeling is only partially justified by the facts, since we also know that the unconscious is capable of producing beneficial effects. The kind of effect it will have depends to a large extent on the attitude of the conscious mind.

Hence the *mundificatio*—purification—is an attempt to discriminate the mixture, to sort out the *coincidentia oppositorum* in which the individual has been caught. The rational man, in order to live in this world, has to make a distinction between "himself" and what we might call the "eternal man." Although he is a unique individual, he also stands for "man" as a species, and thus he has a share in all the movements of the collective unconscious. In other words, the "eternal" truths become dangerously disturbing factors when they suppress the unique ego of the individual and live at his expense. If our psychology is forced, owing to the special nature of its empirical material, to stress the importance of the unconscious, that does not in any way diminish the importance of ego-consciousness. It is merely the one-sided over-valuation of the latter that has to be checked by a certain relativization of values. But this relativization should not be carried so far that the ego is completely fascinated and overpowered by the archetypal truths. The ego lives in space and time and must adapt itself to their laws if it is to exist at all. If it is absorbed by the unconscious to such an extent that the latter alone has the power of decision, then the ego is stifled, and there is no longer any medium in which the unconscious could be integrated and in which the work of realization could take place. The separation of the empirical ego from the "eternal" and universal man is therefore of vital importance, particularly today, when mass-degeneration of the personality is making such threatening strides. Mass-degeneration does not come only from without: it also comes from within, from the collective unconscious. Against the outside, some protection was afforded by the *droits de l'homme* which at present are lost to the greater part of Europe,[26] and even where they are not actually lost we see political parties, as naïve

[26] As this book was written in 1943, I leave this sentence as it stands, in the hope of a better world to come.

as they are powerful, doing their best to abolish them in favour of the slave state, with the bait of social security. Against the daemonism from within, the Church offers some protection so long as it wields authority. But protection and security are only valuable when not excessively cramping to our existence; and in the same way the superiority of consciousness is desirable only if it does not suppress and shut out too much life. As always, life is a voyage between Scylla and Charybdis.

The process of differentiating the ego from the unconscious,[27] then, has its equivalent in the *mundificatio,* and, just as this is the necessary condition for the return of the soul to the body, so the body is necessary if the unconscious is not to have destructive effects on the ego-consciousness, for it is the body that gives bounds to the personality. The unconscious can be integrated only if the ego holds its ground. Consequently, the alchemist's endeavour to unite the *corpus mundum,* the purified body, with the soul is also the endeavour of the psychologist once he has succeeded in freeing the ego-consciousness from contamination with the unconscious. In alchemy the purification is the result of numerous distillations; in psychology too it comes from an equally thorough separation of the ordinary ego-personality from all inflationary admixtures of unconscious material. This task entails the most painstaking self-examination and self-education, which can, however, be passed on to others by one who has acquired the discipline himself. The process of psychological differentiation is no light work; it needs the tenacity and patience of the alchemist, who must purify the body from all superfluities in the fiercest heat of the furnace, and pursue Mercurius "from one bride chamber to the next." As alchemical symbolism shows, a radical understanding of this kind is impossible without a human partner. A general and merely academic "insight into one's mistakes" is ineffectual, for then the mistakes are not really seen at all, only the idea of them. But they show up acutely when a human relationship brings them to the fore and when they are noticed by the other person as well as by oneself. Then and then only can they really be felt and their true nature recognized. Similarly, confessions made to one's secret self generally have little

[27] This process is described in the second of my *Two Essays.*

or no effect, whereas confessions made to another are much more promising.

The "soul" which is reunited with the body is the One born of the two, the *vinculum* common to both.[28] It is therefore the very essence of relationship. Equally the psychological anima, as representative of the collective unconscious, has a collective character. The collective unconscious is a natural and universal datum and its manifestation always causes an unconscious identity, a state of *participation mystique*. If the conscious personality becomes caught up in it and offers no resistance, the relationship is personified by the anima (in dreams, for instance), who then, as a more or less autonomous part of the personality, generally has a disturbing effect. But if, as the result of a long and thorough analysis and the withdrawal of projections, the ego has been successfully separated from the unconscious, the anima will gradually cease to act as an autonomous personality and will become a function of relationship between conscious and unconscious. So long as she is projected she leads to all sorts of illusions about people and things and thus to endless complications. The withdrawal of projections makes the anima what she originally was: an archetypal image which, in its right place, functions to the advantage of the individual. Interposed between the ego and the world, she acts like an ever-changing Shakti, who weaves the veil of Maya and dances the illusion of existence. But, functioning between the ego and the unconscious, the anima becomes the matrix of all the divine and semi-divine figures, from the pagan goddess to the Virgin, from the messenger of the Holy Grail to the saint.[29] The unconscious anima is a creature without relationships, an autoerotic being whose one aim is to take total possession of the individual. When this happens to a man he becomes strangely womanish in the worst sense, with a moody and uncontrolled disposition which, in time, has a deleterious effect

[28] Cf. "Tractatulus Aristotelis," *Art. aurif.*, I, p. 371.

[29] A good example of this is to be found in Angelus Silesius, *Cherubinischer Wandersmann*, Book III, no. 238:

> "God is made man and now is born—rejoice!
> Where then? In me, the mother of his choice.
> How should that be? My soul that Virgin Maid,
> My heart the manger and my limbs the shed. . . ."

even on the hitherto reliable functions—e.g., his intellect—and gives rise to the kind of ideas and opinions we rightly find so objectionable in animus-possessed women.[30]

Here I must point out that very different rules apply in feminine psychology, since in this case we are not dealing with a function of relationship but, on the contrary, with a *discriminative* function, namely the animus. Alchemy was, as a philosophy, mainly a masculine preoccupation and in consequence of this its formulations are for the most part masculine in character. But we should not overlook the fact that the feminine element in alchemy is not so inconsiderable since, even at the time of its beginnings in Alexandria, we have authentic proof of female philosophers like Theosebeia,[31] the *soror mystica* of Zosimos, and Paphnutia and Maria Prophetissa. From later times we know of the pair of alchemists, Nicolas Flamel and his wife Peronelle. The *Mutus liber* of 1677 gives an account of a man and wife performing the *opus* together,[32] and finally in the nineteenth century we have the pair of English alchemists, Thomas South and his daughter, who later became Mrs. Atwood. After busying themselves for many years with the study of alchemy, they decided to set down their ideas and experiences in book form. To this end they separated, the father working in one part of the house and his daughter in another. She wrote a thick, erudite tome while he versified. She was the first to finish and promptly sent the book to the printer. Scarcely had it appeared when her father was overcome with scruples, fearing lest they had betrayed the great secret. He succeeded in persuading his daughter to withdraw the book and destroy it. In the same spirit, he sacrificed his own poetic labours. Only a few lines are preserved in her book, of which it was too late to withdraw all the copies. A reprint,[33] prepared after her death

[30] In woman the animus produces very similar illusions, the only difference being that they consist of dogmatic opinions and prejudices which are taken over at random from somebody else and are never the product of her own reflection.

[31] She is the Euthicia of the treatise of Rosinus (= Zosimos) in *Art. aurif.*, I, pp. 277ff.

[32] The *Mutus liber* is reproduced as an appendix to Vol. I of the *Bibl. chem. curiosa*, 1702. For illustrations from the *Mutus Liber,* see figs. 11–13 of the present volume, and *Psychology and Alchemy*, index. We might mention John Pordage and Jane Leade (17th cent.) as another pair of alchemists. See infra.

[33] *A Suggestive Inquiry into the Hermetic Mystery.*

n 1910, appeared in 1918. I have read the book: no secrets are
betrayed. It is a thoroughly medieval production garnished
with would-be theosophical explanations as a sop to the syncre-
ism of the new age.

A remarkable contribution to the role of feminine psychology in alchemy is furnished by the letter which the English
theologian and alchemist, John Pordage,[34] wrote to his *soror
mystica* Jane Leade. In it [35] he gives her spiritual instruction
concerning the *opus:*

This sacred furnace, this *Balneum Mariae,* this glass phial, this
secret furnace, is the place, the matrix or womb, and the centre from
which the divine Tincture flows forth from its source and origin.
Of the place or abode where the Tincture has its home and dwelling
I need not remind you, nor name its name, but I exhort you only
to knock at the foundation. Solomon tells us in his Song that its
inner dwelling its not far from the navel, which resembles a round
goblet filled with the sacred liquor of the pure Tincture.[36] You
know the fire of the philosophers, it was the key they kept concealed. . . . The fire is the love-fire, the life that flows forth from
the Divine Venus, or the Love of God; the fire of Mars is too chol-
ric, too sharp, and too fierce, so that it would dry up and burn the
materia: wherefore the love-fire of Venus alone has the qualities of
the right true fire.

This true philosophy will teach you how you should know
yourself, and if you know yourself rightly, you will also know
the pure nature; for the pure nature is in yourself. And when
you know the pure nature which is your true selfhood, freed from
all wicked, sinful selfishness, then also you will know God, for the

---

[34] John Pordage (1607–1681) studied theology and medicine in Oxford. He was a
disciple of Jakob Boehme and a follower of his alchemical theosophy. He became
an accomplished alchemist and astrologer. One of the chief figures in his mystical
philosophy is Sophia. ("She is my divine, eternal, essential self-sufficiency. She is
my wheel within my wheel," etc.—Pordage's *Sophia*, p. 21.)

[35] The letter is printed in Roth-Scholtz, *Deutsches Theatrum chemicum*, I, pp.
557–97. The first German edition of this "Philosóphisches Send-Schreiben vom
Stein der Weissheit" seems to have been published in Amsterdam in 1698. [The
letter was evidently written in English, since the German version in Roth-Scholtz,
728–32, is stated to be "aus dem Englischen übersetzet." But no English edition
or MS. can be traced at the British Museum, the Library of Congress, or any of
the other important British and American libraries. Pordage's name does not
occur among the alumni at Oxford.—EDITORS.]

[36] One of the favourite allusions to the Song of Songs 7:2: "Thy navel is like a
round goblet, which wanteth not liquor." Cf. also *Aurora consurgens*, I, Ch. XII.

Godhead is concealed and wrapped in the pure nature like a kernel in the nutshell. . . . The true philosophy will teach you who is the father and who is the mother of this magical child. . . . The father of this child is Mars, he is the fiery life which proceeds from Mars as the father's quality. His mother is Venus, who is the gentle love-fire proceeding from the son's quality. Here then, in the qualities and forms of nature, you see male and female, man and wife, bride and bridegroom, the first marriage or wedding of Galilee which is celebrated between Mars and Venus when they return from their fallen state. Mars, or the husband, must become a godly man, otherwise the pure Venus will take him neither into the conjugal nor into the sacred marriage bed. Venus must become a pure virgin, a virginal wife, otherwise the wrathful jealous Mars in his wrath-fire will not wed with her nor live with her in union; but instead of agreement and harmony, there will be naught but strife, jealousy, discord, and enmity among the qualities of nature. . .

Accordingly, if you think to become a learned artist, look with earnestness to the union of your own Mars and Venus, that the nuptial knot be rightly tied and the marriage between them well and truly consummated. You must see to it that they lie together in the bed of their union and live in sweet harmony; then the virgin Venus will bring forth her pearl, her water-spirit, in you, to soften the fiery spirit of Mars, and the wrathful fire of Mars will sink quite willingly, in mildness and love, into the love-fire of Venus, and thus both qualities, *as fire and water,* will mingle together, agree, and flow into one another; and from their agreement and union there will proceed the first conception of the magical birth which we call Tincture, the love-fire Tincture. Now although the Tincture is conceived in the womb of your humanity and is awakened to life, yet there is still a great danger, and it is to be feared that, because it is still in the body or womb, it may yet be spoiled by neglect before it be brought in due season into the light. On this account you must look round for a good nurse, who will watch it in its childhood and will tend it properly: and such must be your own pure heart and your own virginal will. . . .

This child, this tincturing life, must be assayed, proved, and tried in the qualities of nature; and here again great anxiety and danger will arise, seeing that it must suffer the damage of temptation in the body and womb, and you may thus lose the birth. For the delicate Tincture, this tender child of life, must descend into the forms and qualities of nature, that it may suffer and endure temptation and overcome it; it must needs descend into the Divine Darkness, into the darkness of Saturn, wherein no light of life is to be seen there it must be held captive, and be bound with the chains of darkness, and must live from the food which the prickly Mercurius will give it to eat, which to the Divine Tincture of life is naught but dust and ashes, poison and gall, fire and brimstone. It must enter into the fierce wrathful Mars, by whom (as happened to Jonah in the belly of hell) it is swallowed, and must experience the curse of God's wrath; also it must be tempted by Lucifer and the million devils who dwell in the quality of the wrathful fire. And here the divine artist in this philosophical work will see the first colour, where the Tincture appears in its blackness, and it is the blackest black; the learned philosophers call it their black crow, or their black raven, or again their blessed and blissful black; for in the darkness of this black is hidden the light of lights in the quality of Saturn; and in this poison and gall there is hidden in Mercurius the most precious medicament against the poison, namely the life of life. And the blessed Tincture is hidden in the fury or wrath and curse of Mars.

Now it seems to the artist that all his work is lost. What has become of the Tincture? Here is nothing that is apparent, that can be perceived, recognized, or tasted, but darkness, most painful death, a hellish fearful fire, nothing but the wrath and curse of God; yet he does not see that the Tincture of Life is in this putrefaction or dissolution and destruction, that there is light in this darkness, life in this death, love in this fury and wrath, and in this poison the highest and most precious Tincture and medicament against all poison and sickness.

The old philosophers named this work or labour their descension, their cineration, their pulverization, their death, their putrefaction of the *materia* of the stone, their corruption, their *caput mortuum*. You must not despise this blackness, or black colour, but persevere in it in patience, in suffering, and in silence, until its forty days of temptation are over, until the days of its tribulations are completed, when the seed of life shall waken to life, shall rise up, sublimate or glorify itself, transform itself into whiteness, purify and sanctify itself, give itself the redness, in other words, transfigure and fix its shape. When the work is brought thus far, it is an easy work: for the learned philosophers have said that the making of the stone is then woman's work and child's play. Therefore, if the human will is given over and left, and becomes patient and still and as a dead nothing, the Tincture will do and effect everything in us and for us, if we can keep our thoughts, movements, and imaginations still, or can leave off and rest. But how difficult, hard, and bitter this work appears to the human will, before it can be brought to this shape, so that it remains still and calm even though all the fire be let loose in its sight, and all manner of temptations assail it!

Here, as you see, there is great danger, and the Tincture of life can easily be spoiled and the fruit wasted in the womb, when it is thus surrounded on all sides and assailed by so many devils and so many tempting essences. But if it can withstand and overcome this fiery trial and sore temptation, and win the victory: then you will see the beginning of its resurrection from hell, death, and the mortal grave, appearing first in the quality of Venus; and then the Tincture of life will itself burst forth mightily from the prison of the dark Saturn, through the hell of the poisonous Mercurius, and through the curse and direful death of God's wrath that burns and flames in Mars, and the gentle love-fire of the Venus quality will gain the upper hand, and the love-fire Tincture will be preferred in the government and have supreme command. And then the gentleness and love-fire of Divine Venus will reign as lord and king in and over all qualities.

Nevertheless there is still another danger that the work of the stone may yet miscarry. Therefore the artist must wait until he sees the Tincture covered over with its other colour, as with the whitest white, which he may expect to see after long patience and stillness, and which truly appears when the Tincture rises up in the lunar quality: illustrious Luna imparts a beautiful white to the Tincture, the most perfect white hue and a brilliant splendour. And thus is the darkness transformed into light, and death into life. And this brilliant whiteness awakens joy and hope in the heart of the artist, that the work has gone so well and fallen out so happily. For now the white colour reveals to the enlightened eye of the soul cleanliness, innocence, holiness, simplicity, heavenly-mindedness, and righteousness, and with these the Tincture is henceforth clothed over and over as with a garment. She is radiant as the moon, beautiful as the dawn. Now the divine virginity of the tincturing life shines forth, and no spot or wrinkle nor any other blemish is to be seen.

The old masters were wont to call this work their white swan, their albification, or making white, their sublimation, their distillation, their circulation, their purification, their separation, their sanctification, and their resurrection, because the Tincture is made white like a shining silver. It is sublimed or exalted and transfigured by reason of its many descents into Saturn, Mercurius, and Mars, and by its many ascents into Venus and Luna. This is the distillation, the *Balneum Mariae:* because the Tincture is purified in the qualities of nature through the many distillations of the water, blood, and heavenly dew of the Divine Virgin Sophia, and, hrough the manifold circulation in and out of the forms and qualiies of nature, is made white and pure, like brilliantly polished silver. And all uncleanliness of the blackness, all death, hell, curse, wrath, and all poison which rise up out of the qualities of Saturn, Mercury, and Mars are separated and depart, wherefore they call it their separation, and when the Tincture attains its whiteness and brilliance in Venus and Luna they call it their sanctification, their purification and making white. They call it their resurrection, because the white rises up out of the black, and the divine virginity and purity out of the poison of Mercurius and out of the red fiery rage and wrath of Mars. . . .

Now is the stone shaped, the elixir of life prepared, the lovechild or the child of love born, the new birth completed, and the work made whole and perfect. Farewell! fall, hell, curse, death, dragon, beast, and serpent! Good night! mortality, fear, sorrow, and misery! For now redemption, salvation, and recovery of everything that was lost will again come to pass within and without, for now you have the great secret and mystery of the whole world; you have the Pearl of Love; you have the unchangeable eternal essence of Divine Joy from which all healing virtue and all multiplying power come, from which there actively proceeds the active power of the Holy Ghost. You have the seed of the woman who has trampled on the head of the serpent. You have the seed of the virgin and the blood of the virgin in one essence and quality.

O wonder of wonders! You have the tincturing Tincture, the pearl of the virgin, which has three essences or qualities in one; it has body, soul, and spirit, it has fire, light, and joy, it has the Father's quality, it has the Son's quality, and has also the Holy Ghost's quality, even all these three, in one fixed and eternal essence and being. This is the Son of the Virgin, this is her first-born, this is the noble hero, the trampler of the serpent, and he who casts the dragon under his feet and tramples upon him. . . . For now the Man of Paradise is become clear as a transparent glass, in which the Divine Sun shines through and through, like gold that is wholly bright, pure, and clear, without blemish or spot. The soul is henceforth a most substantial seraphic angel, she can make herself doctor, theologian, astrologer, divine magician, she can make herself whatsoever she will, and do and have whatsoever she will: for all qualities have but one will in agreement and harmony. And this same one will is God's eternal infallible will; and from henceforth the Divine Man is in his own nature become one with God.[37]

37 The concluding passages are very reminiscent of the teachings of the "secta liberi spiritus," which were propagated as early as the 13th century by the Béguines and Beghards.

This hymn-like myth of love, virgin, mother, and child sounds extremely feminine, but in reality it is an archetypal conception sprung from the masculine unconscious, where the Virgin Sophia corresponds to the anima (in the psychological sense).[38] As is shown by the symbolism and by the not very clear distinction between her and the son, she is also the "paradisal" or "divine" being, i.e., the self. The fact that these ideas and figures were still mystical for Pordage and more or less undifferentiated is explained by the emotional nature of the experiences which he himself describes.[39] Experiences of this kind leave little room for critical understanding. They do, however, throw light on the processes hidden behind the alchemical symbolism and pave the way for the discoveries of modern medical psychology. Unfortunately we possess no original treatises that can with any certainty be ascribed to a woman author. Consequently we do not know what kind of alchemical symbolism a woman's view would have produced. Nevertheless, modern medical practice tells us that the feminine unconscious produces a symbolism which, by and large, is compensatory to the masculine. In that case, to use Pordage's terms, the leitmotiv would not be gentle Venus but fiery Mars, not Sophia but Hecate, Demeter, and Persephone, or the matriarchal Kali of southern India in her brighter and darker aspects.[40]

In this connection I would like to draw attention to the curious pictures of the *arbor philosophica* in the fourteenth-century Codex Ashburnham.[41] One picture shows Adam struck by an arrow,[42] and the tree growing out of his genitals; in the

[38] Hence Pordage's view is more or less in agreement with woman's conscious psychology, but not with her unconscious psychology.

[39] Pordage, *Sophia*, Ch. I.

[40] There is a modern work that gives an excellent account of the feminine world of symbols: Esther Harding's *Woman's Mysteries*.

[41] Florence, Ashburnham 1166, 14th cent. They are reproduced as figs. 131 and 135 in *Psychology and Alchemy*.

[42] The arrow refers to the *telum passionis* of Mercurius. Cf. "Cantilena Riplaei" in ibid., par. 491, and *Mysterium Coniunctionis*, pp. 285ff. Cf. also "The Spirit Mercurius," Part II, sec. 8, and St. Bernard of Clairvaux, *Sermones in Cantica* XXX, 8 (Migne, *P.L.*, vol. 183, cols. 932–33): "Est et sagitta sermo Dei vivus et efficax et penetrabilior omni gladio ancipiti. . . . Est etiam sagitta electa amor Christi, quae Mariae animam non modo confixit, sed etiam pertransivit, ut nullam in pectore virginali particulam vacuam amore relinqueret." (God's word is an arrow; it is lively and effective and more penetrating than a double-edged

other picture the tree grows out of Eve's head. Her right hand covers her genitals, her left points to a skull. Plainly this is a hint that the man's *opus* is concerned with the erotic aspect of the anima, while the woman's is concerned with the animus, which is a "function of the head." [43] The *prima materia*, i.e., the unconscious, is represented in man by the "unconscious" anima, and in woman by the "unconscious" animus. Out of the *prima materia* grows the philosophical tree, the unfolding *opus*. In their symbolical sense, too, the pictures are in accord with the findings of psychology, since Adam would then stand for the woman's animus who generates "philosophical" ideas with his member (λόγοι σπερματικοί), and Eve for the man's anima who, as Sapientia or Sophia, produces out of her head the intellectual content of the work.

Finally, I must point out that a certain concession to feminine psychology is also to be found in the *Rosarium*, in so far as the first series of pictures is followed by a second—less complete, but otherwise analogous—series, at the end of which there appears a masculine figure, the "emperor," and not, as in the first, an "empress," the "daughter of the philosophers." The accentuation of the feminine element in the Rebis (Fig. 10) is consistent with a predominantly male psychology, whereas the addition of an "emperor" in the second version is a concession to woman (or possibly to the male consciousness).

In its primary "unconscious" form the animus is a compound of spontaneous, unpremeditated opinions which exercise a powerful influence on the woman's emotional life, while the anima is similarly compounded of feelings which thereafter influence or distort the man's understanding ("she has turned his head"). Consequently the animus likes to project himself upon "intellectuals" and all kinds of "heroes," including tenors, artists, sporting celebrities, etc. The anima has a predilection for everything that is unconscious, dark, equivocal, and un-

---

sword. . . . And the love of Christ is a choice arrow too, which not only entered, but transfixed, the soul of Mary, so that it left no particle of her virgin heart free of love.)—Trans. by a priest of Mount Melleray, I, p. 346.

43 Cf. the Alaskan Eskimo tale "The Woman Who Became a Spider," in Rasmussen, *Die Gabe des Adlers*, pp. 121ff., and the Siberian tale "The Girl and the Skull," in Kunike (ed.), *Märchen aus Sibirien*, No. 31, where a woman marries a skull.

related in woman, and also for her vanity, frigidity, helplessness, and so forth. In both cases the incest element plays an important part: there is a relation between the young woman and her father, the older woman and her son, the young man and his mother, the older man and his daughter.

It will be clear from all this that the "soul" which accrues to ego-consciousness during the *opus* has a feminine character in the man and a masculine character in the woman. His anima wants to reconcile and unite; her animus tries to discern and discriminate. This strict antithesis is depicted in the alchemists' Rebis, the symbol of transcendental unity, as a coincidence of opposites; but in conscious reality—once the conscious mind has been cleansed of unconscious impurities by the preceding *mundificatio*—it represents a conflict even though the conscious relations between the two individuals may be quite harmonious. Even when the conscious mind does not identify itself with the inclinations of the unconscious, it still has to face them and somehow take account of them in order that they may play their part in the life of the individual, however difficult this may be. For if the unconscious is not allowed to express itself through word and deed, through worry and suffering, through our consideration of its claims and resistance to them, then the earlier, divided state will return with all the incalculable consequences which disregard of the unconscious may entail. If, on the other hand, we give in to the unconscious too much, it leads to a positive or negative inflation of the personality. Turn and twist this situation as we may, it always remains an inner and outer conflict: one of the birds is fledged and the other not. We are always in doubt: there is a pro to be rejected and a contra to be accepted. All of us would like to escape from this admittedly uncomfortable situation, but we do so only to discover that what we left behind us was ourselves. To live in perpetual flight from ourselves is a bitter thing, and to live with ourselves demands a number of Christian virtues which we then have to apply to our own case, such as patience, love, faith, hope, and humility. It is all very fine to make our neighbour happy by applying them to him, but the demon of self-admiration so easily claps us on the back and says, "Well done!" And because this is a great psychological truth, it must be stood on its head for an equal number of people so as to give the devil something to carp at. But—does it make *us* happy when we have to apply these virtues to ourselves? when I am the recipient of my own gifts, the least among my brothers whom I must take to my bosom? when I must admit that I need all my patience, my love, my faith, and even my humility, and that I myself am my own devil, the antagonist who always wants the opposite in everything? Can we ever really endure ourselves? "Do unto others . . ."—this is as true of evil as of good.

In John Gower's *Confessio amantis* [44] there is a saying which I have used as a motto to the Introduction of this book: "Bellica pax, vulnus dulce, suave malum" (a warring peace, a sweet wound, a mild evil). Into these words the old alchemist put the quintessence of his experience. I can add nothing to their incomparable simplicity and conciseness. They contain all that the ego can reasonably demand of the *opus,* and illuminate for it the paradoxical darkness of human life. Submission to the fundamental contrariety of human nature amounts to an acceptance of the fact that the psyche is at cross purposes with itself. Alchemy teaches that the tension is fourfold, forming a cross which stands for the four warring elements. The quaternio is the minimal aspect under which such a state of total opposition can be regarded. The cross as a form of suffering expresses psychic reality, and carrying the cross is therefore an apt symbol for the wholeness and also for the passion which the alchemist saw in his work. Hence the *Rosarium* ends, not unfittingly, with the picture of the risen Christ and the verses:

> After my many sufferings and great martyry
> I rise again transfigured, of all blemish free.

An exclusively rational analysis and interpretation of alchemy, and of the unconscious contents projected into it, must necessarily stop short at the above parallels and antinomies, for in a total opposition there is no third—*tertium non datur!* Science comes to a stop at the frontiers of logic, but nature does not—she thrives on ground as yet untrodden by theory. *Venerabilis natura* does not halt at the opposites; she uses them to create, out of opposition, a new birth.

[44] Ed. Macaulay, II, p. 35: motto of Book I. Cf. St. Bernard of Clairvaux, *Sermones in Cant.*, XXIX, 8 (Migne, *P.L.*, vol. 183, col. 933) (of Mary): "Et illa quidem in tota se grande et suave amoris vulnus accepit . . ." (And she indeed received a great and sweet wound of love in all her being).

10

THE NEW BIRTH

Here is born the Empress of all honour/
The philosophers name her their daughter.
She multiplies/ bears children ever again/
They are incorruptibly pure and without stain.

[*Figure 10*]

Our last picture is the tenth in the series, and this is certainly no accident, for the denarius is supposed to be the perfect number.[1] We have shown that the axiom of Maria consists of 4, 3, 2, 1; the sum of these numbers is 10, which stands for unity on a higher level. The unarius represents unity in the

---

[1] "Numerus perfectus est denarius" (the perfect number is ten).—Mylius, *Phil. ref.*, p. 134. The Pythagoreans regarded the δεκάς as the τέλειος ἀριθμός.—Hippolytus, *Elenchos*, I, 2, 8. Cf. Joannes Lydus, *De mensibus*, 3, 4, and Proclus, *In Platonis Timaeum Commentaria*, 21 AB. This view was transmitted to alchemy through the *Turba* (pp. 300ff., "Sermo Pythagorae"). Dorn ("Congeries," *Theatr. chem.* I, p. 622) says: "Quando quidem ubi Quaternarius et Ternarius ad Denarium ascendunt, eorum fit ad unitatem regressus. In isto concluditur arcano omnis occulta rerum sapientia." (When the number four and the number three ascend to the number ten, they return to the One. In this secret all the hidden wisdom of things is contained.) But he denies ("Duellum animi," (*Theatr. chem.*, I, p. 545) that $1 + 2 + 3 + 4 = 10$, since 1 is not a number, maintaining that the denarius comes from $2 + 3 + 4 = 9 + 1$. He insists on the elimination of the devilish binarius (ibid., pp. 542ff.). John Dee ("Monas hieroglyphica," *Theatr. chem.*, II, p. 220) derives the denarius in the usual way: the *antiquissimi Latini philosophi* assumed that the *crux rectilinea* meant the denarius. The old author Artefius (probably an Arab) also derives the denarius by adding together the first four numbers ("Clavis", *Theatr. chem.*, IV, p. 222). But later he says that 2 is the first number, and he proceeds to make the following operation: $2 + 1 = 3$, $2 + 2 = 4$, $4 + 1 = 5$, $4 + 3 = 7$, $7 + 1 = 8$, $8 + 1 = 9$, $8 + 2 = 10$, and says that "eodem modo centenarii ex denariis, millenarii vero ex centenariis procreantur" (in the same way the hundreds are produced out of the tens, and the thousands out of the hundreds). This operation can be regarded as either enigmatic or childish.

Hie ist geboren die eddele Keyserin reich/
Die meister nennen sie jhrer dochter gleich.
Die vermeret sich/gebiert kinder ohn zal/
Sein vndötlich rein/vnnd ohn alles mahl.

Die

Figure 10

form of the *res simplex,* i.e., God as *auctor rerum,*[2] while the denarius is the result of the completed work. Hence the real meaning of the denarius is the Son of God.[3] Although the alchemists call it the *filius philosophorum,*[4] they use it as a Christ-symbol and at the same time employ the symbolic qualities of the ecclesiastical Christ-figure to characterize their Rebis.[5] It is probably correct to say that the medieval Rebis had these Christian characteristics, but for the Hermaphroditus of Arabic and Greek sources we must conjecture a partly pagan tradition. The Church symbolism of *sponsus* and *sponsa* leads to the mystic union of the two, i.e., to the *anima Christi* which lives in the *corpus mysticum* of the Church. This unity underlies the idea of Christ's androgyny, which medieval alchemy exploited for its own ends. The much older figure of the Hermaphroditus, whose outward aspect probably derives from a Cyprian *Venus barbata,* encountered in the Eastern Church the already extant idea of an androgynous Christ, which is no doubt connected with the Platonic conception of the bisexual First Man, for Christ is ultimately the Anthropos.

The denarius forms the *totius operis summa,* the culminating point of the work beyond which it is impossible to go except by means of the *multiplicatio.* For, although the denarius represents a higher stage of unity, it is also a multiple of 1 and can therefore be multiplied to infinity in the ratio

---

[2] According to Hippolytus (*Elenchos,* IV, 43, 4), the Egyptians said that God was a μονὰς ἀδιαίρετος (an indivisible unity), and that 10 was a monad, the beginning and end of all number.

[3] The denarius as an *allegoria Christi* is to be found in Rabanus Maurus, *Allegoriae in universam sanctam Scripturam* (Migne, *P.L.,* vol. 112, col. 907).

[4] "Audi atque attende: Sal antiquissimum Mysterium! Cuius nucleum in Denario, Harpocratice, sile." (Listen and pay heed: Salt is the oldest mystery. Hide its nucleus in the number ten, after the manner of Harpocrates.)—Khunrath, *Amphitheatrum,* p. 194. The salt is the salt of wisdom. Harpocrates is the genius of the secret mysteries. Cf. *Psychology and Alchemy,* figs. 52 and 253.

[5] There is a parallel to this in the system of Monoïmos (Hippolytus, *Elenchos,* VIII, 12, 2ff.). The son of Oceanus (the Anthropos) is an indivisible monad and yet divisible: he is mother and father, a monad that is also a decad. "Ex denario divino statues unitatem" (Out of the divine number ten you will constitute unity).—Quotation from Joh. Dausten in Aegidius de Vadis, "Dialogus," *Theatr. chem.,* II, p. 115. Dausten, or Dastyne, was probably an Englishman; certain authorities date him at the beginning of the 14th cent., others much later. See Ferguson, *Bibl. chem.,* I, s.v. "Dausten."

of 10, 100, 1000, 10,000, etc., just as the mystical body of the Church is composed of an indefinitely large number of believers and is capable of multiplying that number without limit. Hence the Rebis is described as the *cibus sempiternus* (everlasting food), *lumen indeficiens,* and so forth; hence also the assumption that the tincture replenishes itself and that the work need only be completed once and for all time.[6] But, since the *multiplicatio* is only an attribute of the denarius, 100 is no different from and no better than 10.[7]

The *lapis,* understood as the cosmogonic First Man, is the *radix ipsius,* according to the *Rosarium*: everything has grown from this One and through this One.[8] It is the Uroboros, the serpent that fertilizes and gives birth to itself, by definition an *increatum,* despite a quotation from Rosarius to the effect that "Mercurius noster nobilissimus" was created by God as a "res nobilis." This *creatum increatum* can only be listed as another paradox. It is useless to rack our brains over this extraordinary attitude of mind. Indeed we shall continue to do so only while we assume that the alchemists were not being consciously and intentionally paradoxical. It seems to me that theirs was a perfectly natural view: anything unknowable could best be described in terms of opposites.[9] A longish poem in German, evidently written at about the time it was printed in the 1550 *Rosarium,* explains the nature of the Hermaphroditus as follows:

> Here is born the Empress of all honour/
> The philosophers name her their daughter.
> She multiplies/ bears children ever again/
> They are incorruptibly pure and without stain.

[6] Norton's "Ordinall," *Theatr. chem. britannicum,* p. 48. Philalethes ("Fons chemicae veritatis," *Mus. herm.,* p. 802) says: "Qui semel adeptus est, ad Autumnum sui laboris pervenit" (He who has once found it has reached the harvest time of his work). This is a quotation from Johannes Pontanus, who lived about 1550 and was a physician and professor of philosophy at Königsberg. Cf. Ferguson, *Bibl. chem.,* II, p. 212.

[7] It is worth noting that St. John of the Cross pictures the ascent of the soul in ten stages.

[8] "Ipsa omnia sunt ex uno et de uno et cum uno, quod est radix ipsius" (They are all from the One, and of the One, and with the One, which is the root of itself).—*Art. aurif.,* II, p. 369.

[9] Nicholas of Cusa, in his *De docta ignorantia,* regarded antinomial thought as the highest form of reasoning.

The Queen hates death and poverty
She surpasses gold silver and jewellery/
All medicaments great and small.
Nothing upon earth is her equal/
Wherefore we say thanks to God in heaven.
O force constrains me naked woman that I am/
For unblest was my body when I first began.
And never did I become a mother/
Until the time when I was born another.
Then the power of roots and herbs did I possess/
And I triumphed over all sickness.
Then it was that I first knew my son/
And we two came together as one.
There I was made pregnant by him and gave birth
Upon a barren stretch of earth.
I became a mother yet remained a maid/
And in my nature was establishèd.
Therefore my son was also my father/
As God ordained in accordance with nature.
I bore the mother who gave me birth/
Through me she was born again upon earth.
To view as one what nature hath wed/
Is in our mountain most masterfully hid.
Four come together in one/
In this our magisterial Stone.
And six when seen as a trinity/
Is brought to essential unity.
To him who thinks on these things aright/
God giveth the power to put to flight
All such sicknesses as pertain
To metals and the bodies of men.
None can do that without God's help/
And then only if he see through himself.
Out of my earth a fountain flows/
And into two streams it branching goes.
One of them runs to the Orient/
The other towards the Occident.
Two eagles fly up with feathers aflame/
Naked they fall to earth again.
Yet in full feather they rise up soon/
That fountain is Lord of sun and moon.
O Lord Jesu Christ who bestow'st
The gift through the grace of thy Holy Ghost:

He unto whom it is given truly/
Understands the masters' sayings entirely.
That his thoughts on the future life may dwell/
Body and soul are joined so well.
And to raise them up to their father's kingdom/
Such is the way of art among men.

This poem is of considerable psychological interest. I have already stressed the anima nature of the androgyne. The "un-blessedness" of the "first body" has its equivalent in the disagreeable, daemonic, "unconscious" anima which we considered in the last chapter. At its second birth, that is, as a result of the opus, this anima becomes fruitful and is born together with her son, in the shape of the Hermaphroditus, the product of mother-son incest. Neither fecundation nor birth impairs her virginity.[10] This essentially Christian paradox is connected with the extraordinary *timeless* quality of the unconscious: everything has already happened and is yet unhappened, is already dead and yet unborn.[11] Such paradoxical statements illustrate the potentiality of unconscious contents. In so far as comparisons are possible at all, they are objects of memory and knowledge, and in this sense belong to the remote past; we therefore speak of "vestiges of primordial mythological ideas." But, in so far as the unconscious manifests itself in a sudden incomprehensible invasion, it is something that was never there before, something altogether strange, new, and belonging to the future. The unconscious is thus the mother as well as the daughter, and the mother has given birth to her own mother (*increatum*), and

---

[10] Cf. "Rosinus ad Sarratantam," *Art. aurif.*, I, p. 309: "Cuius [lapidis] mater virgo est, et pater non concubuit" (Its [the stone's] mother is a virgin, and the father lay not with her).

[11] Cf. Petrus Bonus, "Pretiosa margarita novella," *Theatr. chem.*, V, p. 649: "Cuius mater virgo est, cuius pater foeminam nescit. Adhuc etiam noverunt, quod Deus fieri debet homo, quia in die novissima huius artis, in qua est operis complementum, generans et generatum fiunt omnino unum: et senex et puer et pater et filius fiunt omnino unum. Ita quod omnia vetera fiunt nova." (Whose mother is a virgin and whose father knew not woman. They knew also that God must become man, because on the last day of this art, when the completion of the work takes place, begetter and begotten become altogether one. Old man and youth, father and son, become altogether one. Thus all things old are made new.)

her son was her father.[12] It seems to have dawned on the alchemists that this most monstrous of paradoxes was somehow connected with the self, for no man can practise such an art unless
it be with God's help, and unless "he see through himself." The
old masters were aware of this, as we can see from the dialogue
between Morienus and King Kalid. Morienus relates how Her-
cules (the Byzantine Emperor Heraclius) told his pupils: "O
sons of wisdom, know that God, the supreme and glorious
Creator, has made the world out of four unequal elements and
set man as an ornament between them." When the King begged
for further explanation, Morienus answered: "Why should I
tell you many things? For this substance [i.e., the arcanum] is
extracted from you, and you are its ore; in you the philosophers find it, and, that I may speak more plainly, from you they
take it. And when you have experienced this, the love and
desire for it will be increased in you. And you shall know that
this thing subsists truly and beyond all doubt. . . . For in this
stone the four elements are bound together, and men liken it to
the world and the composition of the world." [13]

One gathers from this discourse that, owing to his position between the four world-principles, man contains within
himself a replica of the world in which the unequal elements
are united. This is the microcosm in man, corresponding to the
"firmament" or "Olympus" of Paracelsus: that unknown quan-
tity in man which is as universal and wide as the world itself,
which is in him by nature and cannot be acquired. Psychologically, this corresponds to the collective unconscious, whose
projections are to be found everywhere in alchemy. I must re-
frain from adducing more proofs of the psychological insight of
the alchemists, since this has already been done elsewhere.[14]

The end of the poem hints at immortality—at the great hope
of the alchemists, the *elixir vitae*. As a transcendental idea, immortality cannot be the object of experience, hence there is no
argument either for or against. But immortality as an *experience of feeling* is rather different. A feeling is as indisputable a
reality as the existence of an idea, and can be experienced to

12 Cf. Dante, *Paradiso*, XXXIII, i: "O Virgin Mother, daughter of thy son."
13 "Sermo de transmutatione metallorum," *Art. aurif.*, II, p. 37.
14 Cf. "Psychology and Religion," pars. 95ff., 153ff.; and *Psychology and Alchemy*, pars. 342ff.

exactly the same degree. On many occasions I have observed that the spontaneous manifestations of the self, i.e., the appearance of certain symbols relating thereto, bring with them something of the timelessness of the unconscious which expresses itself in a feeling of eternity or immortality. Such experiences can be extraordinarily impressive. The idea of the *aqua permanens,* the *incorruptibilitas lapidis,* the *elixir vitae,* the *cibus immortalis,* etc., is not so very strange, since it fits in with the phenomenology of the collective unconscious.[15] It might seem a monstrous presumption on the part of the alchemist to imagine himself capable, even with God's help, of producing an everlasting substance. This claim gives many treatises an air of boastfulness and humbug on account of which they have deservedly fallen into disrepute and oblivion. All the same, we should beware of emptying out the baby with the bath water. There are treatises that look deep into the nature of the *opus* and put another complexion on alchemy. Thus the anonymous author of the *Rosarium* says: "It is manifest, therefore, that the stone is the master of the philosophers, as if he [the philosopher] were to say that he does of his own nature that which he is compelled to do; and so the philosopher is not the master, but rather the minister, of the stone. Consequently, he who attempts through the art and apart from nature to introduce into the matter anything which is not in it naturally, errs, and will bewail his error."[16] This tells us plainly enough that the artist does not act from his own creative whim, but is driven to act by the stone. This almighty taskmaster is none other than the self. The self wants to be made manifest in the work, and for this reason the *opus* is a process of individuation, a becoming of the self. The self is the total, timeless man and as such corresponds

[15] It goes without saying that these concepts offer no solution of any metaphysical problem. They neither prove nor disprove the immortality of the soul.
[16] *Art. aurif.,* II, pp. 356f.: "Patet ergo quod Philosophorum Magister lapis est, quasi diceret, quod naturaliter etiam per se facit quod tenetur facere: et sic Philosophus non est Magister lapidis, sed potius minister. Ergo qui quaerit per artem extra naturam per artificium inducere aliquid in rem, quod in ea naturaliter non est, errat et errorem suum deflebit." [The above translation follows the author's German version. An equally likely translation of the "quasi diceret" clause would be: "as if it (the stone) were to say that it does of its own nature that which it is held to do."—A.S.B.G.]

to the original, spherical,[17] bisexual being who stands for the mutual integration of conscious and unconscious.

From the foregoing we can see how the *opus* ends with the idea of a highly paradoxical being that defies rational analysis. The work could hardly end in any other way, since the *complexio oppositorum* cannot possibly lead to anything but a baffling paradox. Psychologically, this means that human wholeness can only be described in antinomies, which is always the case when dealing with a transcendental idea. By way of comparison, we might mention the equally paradoxical corpuscular theory and wave theory of light, although these do at least hold out the possibility of a mathematical synthesis, which the psychological idea naturally lacks. Our paradox, however, offers the possibility of an *intuitive* and *emotional* experience, because the unity of the self, unknowable and incomprehensible, irradiates even the sphere of our discriminating, and hence divided, consciousness, and, like all unconscious contents, does so with very powerful effects. This inner unity, or experience of unity, is expressed most forcibly by the mystics in the idea of the *unio mystica,* and above all in the philosophies and religions of India, in Chinese Taoism, and in the Zen Buddhism of Japan. From the point of view of psychology, the names we give to the self are quite irrelevant, and so is the question of whether or not it is "real." Its psychological reality is enough for all practical purposes. The intellect is incapable of knowing anything beyond that anyway, and therefore its Pilate-like questionings are devoid of meaning.

To come back to our picture: it shows an apotheosis of the Rebis, the right side of the body being male, the left female. The figure stands on the moon, which in this case corresponds to the feminine lunar vessel, the *vas hermeticum.* Its wings betoken volatility, i.e., spirituality. In one hand it holds a chalice with three snakes in it, or possibly one snake with three heads; in the other, a single snake. This is an obvious allusion to the axiom of Maria and the old dilemma of 3 and 4, and also to the mystery of the Trinity. The three snakes

[17] The Persian Gayomart is as broad as he is long, hence spherical in shape like the world-soul in Plato's *Timaeus.* He is supposed to dwell in each individual soul and in it to return to God. See Reitzenstein and Schaeder, *Studien zum antiken Synkretismus,* p. 25.

in the chalice are the chthonic equivalent of the Trinity, and the single snake represents, firstly, the unity of the three as expressed by Maria and, secondly, the "sinister" *serpens Mercurialis* with all its subsidiary meanings.[18] Whether pictures of this kind are in any way related to the Baphomet[19] of the Templars is an open question, but the snake symbolism[20] certainly points to the evil principle, which, although excluded from the Trinity, is yet somehow connected with the work of redemption. Moreover to the left of the Rebis we also find the raven, a synonym for the devil.[21] The unfledged bird has disappeared: its place is taken by the winged Rebis. To the right, there stands the "sun and moon tree," the *arbor philosophica,* which is the conscious equivalent of the unconscious process of development suggested on the opposite side. The corresponding picture of the Rebis in the second version[22] has, instead of the raven, a pelican plucking its breast for its young, a well-known allegory of Christ. In the same picture a lion is prowling about behind the Rebis and, at the bottom of the hill on which the Rebis stands, there is the three-headed snake.[23] The alchemical hermaphrodite is a problem in itself and really needs special elucidation. Here I will say only a few words

18 Cf. "The Spirit Mercurius."

19 Possibly from βαφή (*tinctura*) and μῆτις (skill, sagacity), thus roughly corresponding to the Krater of Hermes filled with νοῦς. Cf. Nicolai, *Versuch über die Beschuldigungen, welche dem Tempelherrenorden gemacht wurden,* p. 120; Hammer-Purgstall, *Mysterium Baphometis,* pp. 3ff.

20 Cf. *Psychology and Alchemy,* fig. 70, showing a snake ritual. There is no certain connection of snake worship with the Templars (Hammer-Purgstall, *Mémoire sur deux coffrets gnostiques*).

21 Anastasius Sinaïta, *Anagogicae contemplationes:* "Et cum vel suffocatus esset et perisset tenebrosus corvus Satan . . ." (And when the dark raven Satan [or: of Satan] was suffocated or had perished . . .). St. Ambrose, *De Noe et Arca,* I, 17 (Migne, *P.L.,* vol. 14, col. 411): "Siquidem omnis impudentia atque culpa tenebrosa est et mortuis pascitur sicut corvus . . ." (If indeed all shamelessness and guilt is dark and feeds on the dead like a raven . . .). Again, the raven signifies the sinners: St. Augustine, *Annotationes in Job,* I, xxviii, 41 (Migne, *P.L.,* vol. 34, col. 880): "Significantur ergo nigri [scl. corvi] hoc est peccatores nondum dealbati remissione peccatorum" (They signify the black [raven], i.e., the sinners not yet whitened by remission of their sins). Paulinus of Aquileia, *Liber exhortationis* (Migne, *P.L.,* vol. 99, col. 253): "anima peccatoris . . . quae nigrior corvo est" (The soul of a sinner . . . which is blacker than a raven).

22 *Art. aurif.,* II, p. 359. See *Psychology and Alchemy,* fig. 54.

23 For further pictures of the Rebis see ibid., Index, s.v. "hermaphrodite."

about the remarkable fact that the fervently desired goal of the alchemist's endeavours should be conceived under so monstrous and horrific an image. We have proved to our satisfaction that the antithetical nature of the goal largely accounts for the monstrosity of the corresponding symbol. But this rational explanation does not alter the fact that the monster is a hideous abortion and a perversion of nature. Nor is this a mere accident undeserving of further scrutiny; it is on the contrary highly significant and the outcome of certain psychological facts fundamental to alchemy. The symbol of the hermaphrodite, it must be remembered, is one of the many synonyms for the goal of the art. In order to avoid unnecessary repetition I would refer the reader to the material collected in *Psychology and Alchemy,* and particularly to the lapis-Christ parallel, to which we must add the rarer and, for obvious reasons, generally avoided comparison of the *prima materia* with God.[24] Despite the closeness of the analogy, the *lapis* is not to be understood simply as the risen Christ and the *prima materia* as God; the *Tabula smaragdina* hints, rather, that the alchemical mystery is a "lower" equivalent of the higher mysteries, a sacrament not of the paternal "mind" but of maternal "matter." The disappearance of theriomorphic symbols in Christianity is here compensated by a wealth of allegorical animal forms which tally quite well with *mater natura.* Whereas the Christian figures are the product of spirit, light, and good, the alchemical figures are creatures of night, darkness, poison, and evil. These dark origins do much to explain the misshapen

[24] The identification of the *prima materia* with God occurs not only in alchemy but in other branches of medieval philosophy as well. It derives from Aristotle and its first appearance in alchemy is in the Harranite "Treatise of Platonic Tetralogies" ("Liber Platonis Quartorum," *Theatr. chem.,* V). Mennens ("Aureum vellus," *Theatr. chem.,* V, p. 334) says: "Nomen itaque quadriliterum Dei sanctissimam Trinitatem designare videtur et materiam, quae et umbra eius dicitur et a Moyse Dei posteriora vocatur" (Therefore the four-letter name of God seems to signify the Most Holy Trinity and the Materia, which is also called his shadow, and which Moses called his back parts). Subsequently this idea crops up in the philosophy of David of Dinant, who was attacked by Albertus Magnus. "Sunt quidam haeretici dicentes Deum et materiam primam et νοῦν sive mentem idem esse" (There are some heretics who say that God and the prima materia and the nous or mind are the same thing).—*Summa Theologica,* I, 6, qu. 29, memb. 1, art. 1, par. 5 (*Opera,* ed. Borgnet, vol. 31, p. 294). Further details in Krönlein, "Amalrich von Bena," pp. 303ff.

hermaphrodite, but they do not explain everything. The crude, embryonic features of this symbol express the immaturity of the alchemist's mind, which was not sufficiently developed to equip him for the difficulties of his task. He was underdeveloped in two senses: firstly he did not understand the real nature of chemical combinations, and secondly he knew nothing about the psychological problem of projection and the unconscious. All this lay as yet hidden in the womb of the future. The growth of natural science has filled the first gap, and the psychology of the unconscious is endeavouring to fill the second. Had the alchemists understood the psychological aspects of their work, they would have been in a position to free their "uniting symbol" from the grip of instinctive sexuality where, for better or worse, mere nature, unsupported by the critical intellect, was bound to leave it. Nature could say no more than that the combination of supreme opposites was a hybrid thing. And there the statement stuck, in sexuality, as always when the potentialities of consciousness do not come to the assistance of nature—which could hardly have been otherwise in the Middle Ages owing to the complete absence of psychology.[25] So things remained until, at the end of the nineteenth century, Freud dug up this problem again. There now ensued what usually happens when the conscious mind collides with the unconscious: the former is influenced and prejudiced in the highest degree by the latter, if not actually overpowered by it. The problem of the union of opposites had been lying there for centuries in its sexual form, yet it had to wait until scientific enlightenment and objectivity had advanced far enough for people to mention "sexuality" in scientific conversation. The sexuality of the unconscious was instantly taken with great seriousness and elevated to a sort of religious dogma, which has been fanatically defended right down to the present time: such was the fascination emanating from those contents which had last been nurtured by the alchemists. The natural archetypes that underlie the mythologems of incest, the hierosgamos,

---

[25] The idea of the hermaphrodite is seemingly to be met with in later Christian mysticism. Thus Pierre Poiret (1646–1719), the friend of Mme Guyon, was accused of believing that, in the millennium, propagation would take place hermaphroditically. The accusation was refuted by Cramer (Hauck, *Realencyklopädie*, XV, p. 496), who showed that there was nothing of this in Poiret's writings.

the divine child, etc., blossomed forth—in the age of science—into the theory of infantile sexuality, perversions, and incest, while the *coniunctio* was rediscovered in the transference neurosis.[26]

The sexualism of the hermaphrodite symbol completely overpowered consciousness and gave rise to an attitude of mind which is just as unsavoury as the old hybrid symbolism. The task that defeated the alchemists presented itself anew: how is the profound cleavage in man and the world to be understood, how are we to respond to it and, if possible, abolish it? So runs the question when stripped of its natural sexual symbolism, in which it had got stuck only because the problem could not push its way over the threshold of the unconscious. The sexualism of these contents always denotes an unconscious identity of the ego with some unconscious figure (either anima or animus), and because of this the ego is obliged, willing and reluctant at once, to be a party to the hierosgamos, or at least to believe that it is simply and solely a matter of an erotic consummation. And sure enough it increasingly becomes so the more one believes it—the more exclusively, that is to say, one concentrates on the sexual aspect and the less attention one pays to the archetypal patterns. As we have seen, the whole question invites fanaticism because it is so painfully obvious that we are in the wrong. If, on the other hand, we decline to accept the argument that because a thing is fascinating it is the absolute truth, then we give ourselves a chance to see that the alluring sexual aspect is but one among many—the very one that deludes our judgment. This aspect is always trying to deliver us into the power of a partner who seems compounded of all the qualities we have failed to realize in ourselves. Hence, unless we prefer to be made fools of by our illusions, we shall, by carefully analysing every fascination, extract from it a portion of our own personality, like a quintessence, and slowly come to recognize that we meet ourselves time and again in a thousand disguises on the path of life. This, however, is a truth which only profits the man who is temperamentally convinced of the individual and irreducible reality of his fellow men.

We know that in the course of the dialectical process the

[26] It is interesting to see how this theory once more joined forces with alchemy in Herbert Silberer's book, *Problems of Mysticism and Its Symbolism.*

unconscious produces certain images of the *goal*. In *Psychology and Alchemy* I have described a long series of dreams which contain such images (including even a shooting target). They are mostly concerned with ideas of the mandala type, that is, the circle and the quaternity. The latter are the plainest and most characteristic representations of the goal. Such images unite the opposites under the sign of the quaternio, i.e., by combining them in the form of a cross, or else they express the idea of wholeness through the circle or sphere. The superior type of personality may also figure as a goal-image, though more rarely. Occasionally special stress is laid on the luminous character of the centre. I have never come across the hermaphrodite as a personification of the goal, but more as a symbol of the initial state, expressing an identity with anima or animus.

These images are naturally only anticipations of a wholeness which is, in principle, always just beyond our reach. Also, they do not invariably indicate a subliminal readiness on the part of the patient to realize that wholeness consciously, at a later stage; often they mean no more than a temporary compensation of chaotic confusion and lack of orientation. Fundamentally, of course, they always point to the self, the container and organizer of all opposites. But at the moment of their appearance they merely indicate the possibility of order in wholeness.

What the alchemist tried to express with his Rebis and his squaring of the circle, and what the modern man also tries to express when he draws patterns of circles and quaternities, is wholeness—a wholeness that resolves all opposition and puts an end to conflict, or at least draws its sting. The symbol of this is a *coincidentia oppositorum* which, as we know, Nicholas of Cusa identified with God. It is far from my intention to cross swords with this great man. My business is merely the natural science of the psyche, and my main concern to establish the facts. How these facts are named and what further interpretation is then placed upon them is of secondary importance. Natural science is not a science of words and ideas, but of facts. I am no terminological rigorist—call the existing symbols "wholeness," "self," "consciousness," "higher ego," or what you will, it makes little difference. I for my part only try not to give any false or misleading names. All these terms are sim-

ply names for the facts that alone carry weight. The names
I give do not imply a philosophy, although I cannot prevent
people from barking at these terminological phantoms as if they
were metaphysical hypostases. The facts are sufficient in themselves, and it is well to know about them. But their interpretation should be left to the individual's discretion. "The maximum is that to which nothing is opposed, and in which the
minimum is also the maximum," [27] says Nicholas of Cusa. Yet
God is also above the opposites: "Beyond this coincidence of
creating and being created art thou God." [28] Man is an analogy
of God: "Man is God, but not in an absolute sense, since he is
man. He is therefore God in a human way. Man is also a world,
but he is not all things at once in contracted form, since he is
man. He is therefore a microcosm." [29] Hence the *complexio
oppositorum* proves to be not only a possibility but an ethical
duty: "In these most profound matters every endeavour of our
human intelligence should be bent to the achieving of that
simplicity where contradictories are reconciled." [30] The alchemists are as it were the empiricists of the great problem of the
union of opposites, whereas Nicholas of Cusa is its philosopher.

[27] *De docta ignorantia,* II, 3: "Maximum autem est, cui nihil opponitur, ubi et
Minimum est Maximum."
[28] "Ultra hanc coincidentiam creare cum creari es tu Deus."
[29] *De conjecturis,* II, 14: "Homo enim Deus est, sed non absolute, quoniam
homo. Humane igitur est Deus. Homo etiam mundus est, sed non contracte
omnia, quoniam homo. Est igitur homo μικρόκοσμος."
[30] *Of Learned Ignorance* (trans. Heron), p. 173: "Debet autem in his profundis
omnis nostri humani ingenii conatus esse, ut ad illam se elevet simplicitatem,
ubi contradictoria coincidunt."

EPILOGUE

To give any description of the transference phenomenon is a very difficult and delicate task, and I did not know how to set about it except by drawing upon the symbolism of the alchemical *opus*. The *theoria* of alchemy, as I think I have shown, is for the most part a projection of unconscious contents, of those archetypal forms which are characteristic of all pure fantasy-products, such as are to be met with in myths and fairy-tales, or in the dreams, visions, and the delusional systems of individual men and women. The important part played in the history of alchemy by the hierosgamos and the mystical marriage, and also by the *coniunctio,* corresponds to the central significance of the transference in psychotherapy on the one hand and in the field of normal human relationships on the other. For this reason, it did not seem to me too rash an undertaking to use an historical document, whose substance derives from centuries of mental effort, as the basis and guiding thread of my argument. The gradual unfolding of the symbolic drama presented me with a welcome opportunity to bring together the countless individual experiences I have had in the course of many years' study of this theme—experiences which, I readily admit, I did not know how to arrange in any other way. This venture, therefore, must be regarded as a mere experiment; I have no desire to attribute any conclusive significance to it. The problems connected with the transference are so complicated and so various that I lack the categories necessary for a systematic account. There is in such cases always an urge to simplify things, but this is dangerous because it so easily violates the facts by seeking to reduce incompatibles to a common denominator. I have resisted this temptation so far as possible and allow myself to hope that the reader will not run away with the idea that the process I have described here is a working model of the average course of events. Experience shows, in fact, that not only were the alchemists exceedingly vague as to the sequence of the various stages, but that in our observation of individual cases there is a bewildering number of variations as well as the greatest arbitrariness in the sequence of states, despite all agreement in principle as to the basic facts. A logical order, as we understand it, or even the possibility of such an order, seems to lie outside the bounds of our subject at present. We are moving here in a region of individual and unique happenings that have no parallel. A process of this kind can, if our categories are wide enough, be reduced to an order of sorts and described, or at least adumbrated, with the help of analogies; but its inmost essence is the uniqueness of a life individually lived—which nobody can grasp from outside, but which, on the contrary, holds the individual in its grip. The series of pictures that served as our Ariadne thread is one of many,[1] so that we could easily set up several other working models which would display the process of transference each in a different light. But no single model would be capable of fully expressing the endless wealth of individual variations which all have their *raison d'être*. Such being the case, it is clear to me that even this attempt to give a comprehensive account of the phenomenon is a bold undertaking. Yet its practical importance is so great that the attempt surely justifies itself, even if its defects give rise to misunderstandings.

We live today in a time of confusion and disintegration. Everything is in the melting pot. As is usual in such circumstances, unconscious contents thrust forward to the very borders of consciousness for the purpose of compensating the crisis in which it finds itself. It is therefore well worth our while to examine all such borderline phenomena with the greatest care, however obscure they seem, with a view to discovering the seeds

1 Of these I would draw attention only to the series contained in *Mutus liber,* where the adept and his *soror mystica* are shown performing the *opus.* The first picture (fig. 11) shows an angel waking the sleeper with a trumpet; in the second picture (fig. 12), the pair of alchemists kneel on either side of the Athanor (furnace) with the sealed phial inside it, and above them are two angels holding the same phial, which now contains Sol and Luna, the spiritual equivalents of the two adepts. The third picture (fig. 13) shows, among other things, the soror catching birds in a net and the adept hooking a nixie with rod and line: birds, being volatile creatures, stand for thoughts or the pluralistic animus, and the nixie corresponds to the anima. The undisguisedly psychic character of this portrayal of the *opus* is probably due to the fact that the book was written comparatively late—1677.

Figure 11

Figure 12

Figure 13

of new and potential orders. The transference phenomenon is without doubt one of the most important syndromes in the process of individuation; its wealth of meanings goes far beyond mere personal likes and dislikes. By virtue of its collective contents and symbols it transcends the individual personality and extends into the social sphere, reminding us of those higher human relationships which are so painfully absent in our present social order, or rather disorder. The symbols of the circle and the quaternity, the hallmarks of the individuation process, point back, on the one hand, to the original and primitive order of human society, and forward on the other to an inner order of the psyche. It is as though the psyche were the indispensable instrument in the reorganization of a civilized community as opposed to the collectivities which are so much in favour today, with their aggregations of half-baked mass-men. This type of organization has a meaning only if the human material it purports to organize is good for something. But the mass-man is good for nothing—he is a mere particle that has forgotten what it is to be human and has lost its soul. What our world lacks is the *psychic connection;* and no clique, no community of interests, no political party, and no State will ever be able to replace this. It is therefore small wonder that it was the doctors and not the sociologists who were the first to feel more clearly than anybody else the true needs of man, for, as psychotherapists, they have the most direct dealings with the sufferings of the soul. If my general conclusions sometimes coincide almost word for word with the thoughts of Pestalozzi, the deeper reason for this does not lie in any special knowledge I might possess of this great educator's writings, but in the nature of the subject itself, that is, in insight into the reality of man.

BIBLIOGRAPHY

For the paperback edition of *The Psychology of the Transference* the bibliography of Volume 16 is reproduced in full, inasmuch as only a few of its entries do not apply to this work.

BIBLIOGRAPHY

The items of the bibliography are arranged alphabetically under two
headings: *A*. Ancient volumes containing collections of alchemical
tracts by various authors; *B*. General bibliography, including cross-
references to the material in section *A*. Short titles of the ancient
volumes are printed in capital letters.

A. ANCIENT VOLUMES CONTAINING COLLECTIONS OF ALCHEMICAL TRACTS BY VARIOUS AUTHORS

*ARS CHEMICA, quod sit licita recte exercentibus, probationes doc-
tissimorum iurisconsultorum.* . . . Strasbourg, 1566.

Contents quoted in this volume:

  i   Septem tractatus seu capitula Hermetis Trismegisti aurei
      [pp. 7–31; usually referred to as "Tractatus aureus"]

 ii   Studium Consilii coniugii de massa solis et lunae [pp. 48–
      263; usually referred to as "Consilium coniugii"]

ARTIS AURIFERAE quam chemiam vocant. . . . Basel, [1593].
2 vols.

Contents quoted in this volume:

VOLUME I

   i   Aenigmata ex visione Arislei philosophi et allegoriis sa-
       pientum [pp. 146–54; usually referred to as "Visio
       Arislei"]

  ii   In Turbam philosophorum exercitationes [pp. 154–82]

 iii   Aurora consurgens, quae dicitur Aurea hora [Part II only]
       [pp. 185–246]

  iv   Rosinus ad Euthiciam [pp. 246–77]

   v   Rosinus ad Sarratantam episcopum [pp. 277–319]

  vi   Maria Prophetissa: Practica . . . in artem alchemicam
       [pp. 319–24]

vii   Kalid: Liber secretorum alchemiae [pp. 325–51]

viii Kalid: Liber trium verborum [pp. 352–61]

ix   Tractatulus Aristotelis de practica lapidis philosophici
      [pp. 361–73]

x   Merlinus: Allegoria de arcano lapidis [pp. 392–96]

xi   Tractatulus Avicennae [pp. 405–36]

xii   Liber de arte chimica [pp. 575–631]

VOLUME II

xiii Morienus Romanus: Sermo de transmutatione metallica
      [pp. 7–54]

xiv   Rosarium philosophorum [pp. 204–384]

MANGET(US), JOANNES JACOBUS (ed.). *BIBLIOTHECA CHEMICA
CURIOSA, seu Rerum ad alchemiam pertinentium thesaurus in-
structissimus. . . .* Geneva, 1702. 2 vols.

Contents quoted in this volume:

i   Hermes Trismegistus: Tractatus aureus de lapidis physici
     secreto [pp. 400–445]

ii   Lully: Testamentum novissimum, regi Carolo dicatum
     [pp. 790–806]

iii [Altus:] Mutus Liber, in quo tamen tota Philosophia her-
     metica figuris hieroglyphicis depingitur [pp. 938–53]

*MUSAEUM HERMETICUM reformatum et amplificatum . . . con-
tinens tractatus chimicos XXI praestantissimos . . .* Frankfurt a.
M., 1678. For translation, see (*B*) WAITE.

Contents quoted in this volume:

i   [Hermes Trismegistus:] Tractatus aureus de philoso-
     phorum lapide [pp. 1–52]

ii   [Barcius (F. von Sternberg):] Gloria mundi, alias Paradisi
     tabula [pp. 203–304]

iii Lambspringk: De lapide philosophico figurae et emblem-
     ata [pp. 337–72]

iv   Philalethes: Introitus apertus ad occlusum regis palatium
     [pp. 647–700]

v   Philalethes: Fons chemica veritatis [pp. 799–814]

*THEATRUM CHEMICUM, praecipuos selectorum auctorum trac-
tatus . . . continens.* Vols. I–III, Ursel, 1602; Vols. IV–VI, Strasbourg, 1613, 1622, 1661.

Contents quoted in this volume:

THEATRUM CHEMICUM BRITANNICUM. . . . Collected with annotations by Elias Ashmole. London, 1652.

Contents quoted in this volume:

i Norton: The Ordinall of Alchimy [pp. 13–106; for a modern edition see (*B*) NORTON]

B . GENERAL BIBLIOGRAPHY

ABŪ 'L-QĀSIM. See HOLMYARD.

Acta Joannis (Acts of John). See JAMES.

Adumbratio Kabbalae Christianae. See KNORR VON ROSENROTH.

AEGIDIUS DE VADIS. See *(A) Theatrum chemicum,* **vii.**

AGRIPPA VON NETTESHEIM, HEINRICH CORNELIUS. *De incertitudine et vanitate omnium scientiarum.* The Hague, 1653.

ALBERTUS MAGNUS (Albert the Great, Saint). *Opera omnia.* Ed. Auguste and Emil Borgnet. Paris, 1890–99. 38 vols. ("Summa theologica," vols. 31–35.)

[ALTUS.] *Mutus liber, in quo tamen tota philosophia hermetica figuris hieroglyphicis depingitur.* La Rochelle, 1677. See also *(A) Bibliotheca chemica curiosa,* iii, the source of figs. 11–13.

AMBROSE, SAINT. *De Noe et arca.* See MIGNE, *P.L.,* vol. 14, cols. 381–428.

ANASTASIUS SINAÏTA. *Anagogicae contemplationes in hexaemeron ad Theophilum.* See MIGNE, *P.G.,* vol. 89, cols. 851–1078.

ANDREAE, JOHANN VALENTIN. See ROSENCREUTZ.

ANGELUS SILESIUS (Johannes Scheffler). *Der Cherubinischer Wandersmann.* In: *Sämtliche poetische Werke.* Edited by H. L. Held. Munich, 1924.

Anthropophyteia. Jahrbücher für folkloristische Erhebungen und Forschungen. Edited by Thomas Achelis and others. Leipzig, 1905–12. 9 vols.

ARISTOTLE, pseud. See *(A) Artis auriferae,* **ix;** *(A) Theatrum chemicum,* **xvii.**

ARTEFIUS. See *(A) Theatrum chemicum,* **xii.**

ATWOOD, MARY ANNE. *A Suggestive Inquiry into the Hermetic Mystery.* Belfast, 1920.

AUGUSTINE, SAINT. *Annotationes in Job.* See MIGNE, *P.L.,* vol. 34, cols. 825–86.

———. *The Confessions of Saint Augustine*. Translated by Francis Joseph Sheed. London, 1943.

———. *Epistula LV*. See MIGNE, *P.L.*, vol. 33, cols. 208–09.

"Aurora consurgens."
Part I. See Codices and MSS, iii.
Part II. See *(A) Artis auriferae*, iii.
See also FRANZ, MARIE-LOUISE VON.

AVALON, ARTHUR, pseud. (Sir John Woodroffe) (ed. and trans.). *The Serpent Power*. Translated from the Sanskrit. 3rd revised edn., Madras and London, 1931.

AVICENNA. See *(A) Theatrum chemicum*, xiii; *(A) Artis auriferae*, xi.

Baruch, Apocalypse of. See CHARLES.

BAYNES, CHARLOTTE AUGUSTA. *A Coptic Gnostic Treatise Contained in the Codex Brucianus*. Cambridge, 1933.

BENOÎT, PIERRE. *Atlantida*. Translated by Mary C. Tongue and Mary Ross. [Original: *L'Atlantide*.]

BERNARD OF CLAIRVAUX, SAINT. *Sermones in Cantica Canticorum*. See MIGNE, *P.L.*, vol. 183, cols. 785–1198. For translation, see: *Sermons on the Canticle of Canticles*. Translated by a Priest of Mount Melleray. Dublin, 1920. 2 vols.

BÉROALDE DE VERVILLE, FRANÇOIS. See COLONNA.

BERTHELOT, MARCELLIN. *La Chimie au moyen âge*. (Histoire de sciences.) Paris, 1893. 3 vols.

———. *Collection des anciens alchimistes grecs*. Paris, 1887–88. 3 vols.

BONUS, PETRUS. See *(A) Theatrum chemicum*, xvi.

BOUSSET, WILHELM. *Hauptprobleme der Gnosis*. (Forschungen zur Religion und Literatur des alten und neuen Testaments, X.) Göttingen, 1907.

BROWN, WILLIAM. "The Revival of Emotional Memories and Its Therapeutic Value," *British Journal of Psychology* (London), *Medical Section*, I (1920–21), 16–19.

CARDAN, JEROME (Hieronymus Cardanus). *Somniorum synesiorum omnis generis insomnia explicantes libri IV*. Basel, 1585. 2 vols.

CHARLES, ROBERT HENRY (ed.). *Apocrypha and Pseudepigrapha of the Old Testament*. Oxford, 1913. 2 vols. ("Apocalypse of Baruch," vol. II, pp. 470–526.)

CHRISTENSEN, ARTHUR. *Les Types du premier homme et du premier roi dans l'histoire légendaire des Iraniens.* (Archives d'études orientales, XIV, parts 1–2.) Stockholm, 1917; Leiden, 1934.

CHWOLSOHN, DANIEL ABRAMOVICH. *Die Ssabier und der Ssabismus.* St. Petersburg, 1856. 2 vols.

Codices and Manuscripts:

    i Florence. Biblioteca Medicea-Laurenziana. MS Ashburnham 1166. "Miscellanea d'alchimia." 14th cent.

    ii Paris. Bibliothèque nationale. MS Latin 919. "Grandes heures du duc de Berry." 1413.

    iii Zurich. Zentralbibliothek. Codex Rhenoviensis 172. 15th cent. Item 1: "Aurora consurgens." (Note: Mutilated MS beginning at the fourth parable.)

COLONNA, FRANCESCO. *Hypnerotomachia Poliphili.* . . . Venice, 1499. For French translation, see: *Le Songe de Poliphile.* Translated by François Béroalde de Verville. Paris, 1600. For English paraphrase, see: *The Dream of Poliphilo.* Related and interpreted by Linda Fierz-David. Translated by Mary Hottinger. (Bollingen Series XXV.) New York, 1950.

"Consilium coniugii." See *(A) Ars chemica,* ii.

DEE, JOHN. See *(A) Theatrum chemicum,* ix.

DORN, GERHARD. See *(A) Theatrum chemicum,* ii–v.

DU CANGE, CHARLES DU FRESNE, SIEUR. *Glossarium ad scriptores mediae et infimae graecitatis.* Lyons, 1688. 2 vols.

"Exercitationes in Turbam." See *(A) Artis auriferae,* ii.

FERGUSON, JOHN. *Bibliotheca chemica.* Glasgow, 1906. 2 vols.

FIERZ-DAVID, HANS EDUARD. *Die Entwicklungsgeschichte der Chemie.* Basel, 1945.

FIERZ-DAVID, LINDA. See COLONNA.

FIRMICUS MATERNUS, JULIUS. *Julii Firmici Materni Matheseos Libri VIII.* Ed. W. Kroll and F. Skutsch. Leipzig, 1897–1913. 2 vols. ("Mathesis V. praefatio," vol. II, pp. 1–66.)

FLAMEL, NICHOLAS. See *(A) Theatrum chemicum,* vi.

FRANZ, MARIE-LOUISE VON. *Aurora Consurgens: A Document on the Alchemical Problem of Opposites, Attributed to Thomas Aquinas.*

Translated by R. F. C. Hull and A. S. B. Glover. New York (Bollingen Series) and London, 1966.

FRAZER, SIR JAMES GEORGE. *Taboo and the Perils of the Soul.* (*The Golden Bough*, 3rd edn., vol. III.) London, 1911.

——. *Totemism and Exogamy.* London, 1910. 4 vols.

FREUD, SIGMUND. "Fragment of an Analysis of a Case of Hysteria." Translated by Alix and James Strachey. In: Standard Edn.,* vol. 7. 1953.

——. *Introductory Lectures on Psycho-Analysis.* Translated by James Strachey. Standard Edn.,* vols. 15, 16. 1963.

——. "Leonardo da Vinci and a Memory of His Childhood." Translated by Alan Tyson. In: Standard Edn.,* vol. 11. 1957.

——. "Observations on Transference-Love." Translated by Joan Riviere. In: Standard Edn.,* vol. 12. 1958.

——. "Remembering, Repeating, and Working-Through." Translated by Joan Riviere. In: Standard Edn.,* vol. 12. 1958.

FROBENIUS, LEO. *Das Zeitalter des Sonnengottes.* Berlin, 1904.

"Gloria mundi." See *(A) Musaeum hermeticum,* ii.

GOETHE, JOHANN WOLFGANG VON. *West-östlicher Divan.* For translation, see: *West-Easterly Divan.* Translated with an introduction and notes by J. Weiss. Boston, 1877.

GOODENOUGH, ERWIN. "The Crown of Victory in Judaism," *Art Bulletin* (New York), XXVIII (1926), 135–59.

GOWER, JOHN. *The Complete Works* . . . Edited by G. C. Macaulay. Oxford, 1899–1902. 4 vols. (*Confessio amantis,* vols. II and III.)

GREGORY THE GREAT, SAINT. *Epistolae.* See MIGNE, *P.L.,* vol. 77, cols. 441–1328.

——. *Super Cantica Canticorum Expositio.* See MIGNE, *P.L.,* vol. 79, cols. 471–548.

GUTERMAN, NORBERT (trans.). *Russian Fairy Tales.* London and New York, 1946. (Derived from the original collection of A. N. Afanasiev.)

---

* The Standard Edition of the Complete Psychological Works of Sigmund Freud, translated under the general editorship of James Strachey, in collaboration with Anna Freud, assisted by Alix Strachey and Alan Tyson. London.

HAGGARD, SIR HENRY RIDER. *Ayesha, or The Return of She*. London, 1905.

———. *She*. London, 1887.

HAMMER–PURGSTALL, JOSEPH. *Mémoire sur deux coffrets gnostiques du moyen âge*. Paris, 1835.

———. *Mysterium Baphometis revelatum seu Fratres militiae Templi*. (Fundgruben des Orients, VI.) Vienna, 1818.

HARDING, M. ESTHER. *Woman's Mysteries, Ancient and Modern*. New York, rev. edn., 1955.

HASTINGS, JAMES (ed.). *Encyclopedia of Religion and Ethics*. Edinburgh and New York, 1908–27. 13 vols.

HAUCK, ALBERT (ed.). *Realencyklopädie für protestantische Theologie und Kirche*. Leipzig, 1896–1913. 24 vols.

HERMES TRISMEGISTUS. See "Tractatus aureus."

HIPPOLYTUS. *Elenchos*. In: *Hippolytus Werke*, vol. III. Edited by Paul Wendland. (Die griechische christliche Schriftsteller, XXVI.) Leipzig, 1916.

HOCART, ARTHUR MAURICE. *Kings and Councillors*. Cairo, 1936.

HOGHELANDE, THEOBALD DE. See *(A) Theatrum chemicum*, i.

HOLMYARD, ERIC JOHN. "Abū 'l-Qāsim al-Irāqī," *Isis* (Bruges), VIII (1926), 403–26.

HORTULANUS (Joannes de Garlandia). "Commentarius in Tabulam Smaragdinam Hermetis Trismegisti." In: *De Alchemia*. Nuremberg, 1541. (Pp. 364–73.)

HOWITT, ALFRED WILLIAM. *The Native Tribes of South-East Australia*. London and New York, 1904.

IRENAEUS, SAINT. *Contra (Adversus) haereses*. See MIGNE, *P.G.*, vol. 7, cols. 433–1224. For translation, see: *Five Books of S. Irenaeus . . . against Heresies*. Translated by John Keble. Oxford, 1872.

ISIDORE OF SEVILLE, SAINT. *Liber etymologiarum*. See MIGNE, *P.L.*, vol. 82, cols. 73–728.

JACOBI, JOLANDE. *The Psychology of C. G. Jung*. 6th revised edn., translated by Ralph Manheim. London and New Haven, 1962.

JAMES, MONTAGUE RHODES (ed. and trans.). *The Apocryphal New Testament*. Oxford, 1924. ("Acts of John," pp. 228–70.)

JAMES, WILLIAM. *The Varieties of Religious Experience*. London and New York, 1922.

JEROME, SAINT. *Adversus Jovinianum*. See MIGNE, *P.L.*, vol. 23, cols. 211–338. For translation, see: *Letters and Select Works*. Translated by W. H. Freemantle and others. (Select Library of Nicene and Post-Nicene Fathers.) New York, Oxford, and London, 1893.

John, Acts of. See JAMES, MONTAGUE RHODES.

JOHN OF THE CROSS, SAINT. *The Complete Works.* . . . Translated by E. Allison Peers. London, 1934–35. ("The Dark Night of the Soul," vol. I, pp. 335–486.)

JUNG, CARL GUSTAV. *Aion.* (*Coll. Works,** 9, ii.) 1959; 2nd edn., 1969.

———. "Analytical Psychology and Education." In *Coll. Works,* 17.

———. "Brother Klaus." In *Coll. Works,* 11.

———. "Concerning the Archetypes, with Special Reference to the Anima Concept." In *Coll. Works,* 9, i.

———. "Concerning Mandala Symbolism." In *Coll. Works,* 9, i.

———. *Memories, Dreams, Reflections*. Recorded and edited by Aniela Jaffé. Translated by Richard and Clara Winston. New York and London, 1963. (Edns. separately paginated.)

———. *Mysterium Coniunctionis*. (*Coll. Works,* 14.) 1963.

———. "On Psychic Energy." In *Coll. Works,* 8.

———. "On the Psychology of the Unconscious." In *Coll. Works,* 7.

———. "Paracelsus as a Spiritual Phenomenon." In *Coll. Works,* 13.

———. *Psychological Types*. (*Coll. Works,* 6.*) (Alternative source: *Psychological Types,* translated by H. G. Baynes. London and New York, 1923.)

———. *Psychology and Alchemy*. (*Coll. Works,* 12.) 1953; 2nd edn., 1968.

———. "Psychology and Religion." In *Coll. Works,* 11.

———. "The Relations between the Ego and the Unconscious." In *Coll. Works,* 7.

———. "The Spirit Mercurius." In *Coll. Works,* 13.

* For details of the *Collected Works of C. G. Jung,* including unpublished vols., see list at end of this volume.

JUNG, CARL GUSTAV. "A Study in the Process of Individuation." In *Coll. Works,* 9, i.

———. *Symbols of Transformation.* (*Coll. Works,** 5.) 1956; 2nd edn., 1967.

———. "Synchronicity: An Acausal Connecting Principle." In *Coll. Works,* 8.

———. "The Theory of Psychoanalysis." In *Coll. Works,* 4.

———. *Two Essays on Analytical Psychology.* (*Coll. Works,* 7.) 1953; 2nd edn., 1966.

———. "The Visions of Zosimos." In *Coll. Works,* 13.

KALID. "Liber secretorum alchemiae." See *(A) Artis auriferae,* vii.

———. "Liber trium verborum." See *(A) Artis auriferae,* viii.

KEKULÉ VON STRADONITZ, FRIEDRICH AUGUST. *Lehrbuch der organischen Chemie.* Continued with the co-operation of Richard Anschütz and G. Schultz. Erlangen and Stuttgart, 1861–87. 4 vols.

KERÉNYI, C. (or KARL). *Asklepios: Archetypal Image of the Physician's Existence.* Translated by Ralph Manheim. (Archetypal Images in Greek Religion, 3.) New York (Bollingen Series) and London, 1959.

KHUNRATH, HEINRICH CONRAD. *Amphitheatrum sapientiae aeternae.* Hanau, 1604.

———. *Von hylealischen, das ist, pri-materialischen catholischen, oder algemeinem natürlichen Chaos.* Magdeburg, 1597.

KIRCHER, ATHANASIUS. *Oedipus Aegyptiacus.* Rome, 1652–54. 3. vols.

KLINZ, ALBERT. Ἱερὸς γάμος: *Quaestiones selectae ad sacras nuptias Graecorum religionis et poeseos pertinentes.* Halle, 1933.

KNORR VON ROSENROTH, CHRISTIAN. *Kabbala denudata.* Sulzbach and Frankfurt a. M., 1677–84. 2 vols. (The "Adumbratio kabbalae christianae" is an Appendix to vol. II.)

KOCH, JOSEF (ed.). "Cusanus-Texte," *Sitzungsberichte der Heidelberger Akademie der Wissenschaften, Philosophisch-historische Klasse,* 1936/7, Abh. 2.

KOHUT, ALEXANDER. "Die talmudisch-midraschische Adamssage in ihrer Rückbeziehung auf die persische Yima- und Meshiasage,"

* For details of the *Collected Works of C. G. Jung,* including unpublished vols., see list at end of this volume.

Zeitschrift der Deutschen morgenländischen Gesellschaft (Leipzig), XXV (1871), 59–94.

KRANEFELDT, W. M. "Komplex und Mythos." In: C. G. JUNG and others, *Seelenprobleme der Gegenwart.* 4th edn., Zurich, 1950. (Orig., 1931.)

KRÖNLEIN, J. H. "Amalrich von Bena und David von Dinant," *Theologische Studien und Kritiken* (Hamburg), XXIX (1847), 271ff.

KUNIKE, HUGO (ed.). *Märchen von Sibirien.* (Die Märchen der Weltliteratur.) Jena, 1923.

LAMBSPRINGK. See *(A) Musaeum hermeticum,* iii.

LAVAUD, M. B. *Vie profonde de Nicolas de Flue.* Fribourg, 1942.

LAYARD, JOHN. "The Incest Taboo and the Virgin Archetype," *Eranos-Jahrbuch 1944* (Zurich), XII (1945), 253ff.

———. *Stone Men of Malekula: Vao.* London, 1942.

LEISEGANG, HANS. *Der heilige Geist.* Leipzig, 1919. Vol. I (no more published).

LÉVY-BRUHL, LUCIEN. *How Natives Think.* Translated by Lilian A. Clare (from *Les Fonctions mentales dans les sociétés inférieures*). London, 1926.

"Liber de arte chimica." See *(A) Artis auriferae,* xii.

"Liber Platonis quartorum." See *(A) Theatrum chemicum,* xiv.

LULLY, RAYMUND. "Testamentum." See *(A) Bibliotheca chemica,* ii.

LYDUS, JOANNES (Johannes Laurentius). *De mensibus.* Edited by Richard Wünsch. Leipzig, 1898.

McDOUGALL, WILLIAM. "The Revival of Emotional Memories and its Therapeutic Value," *British Journal of Psychology* (London), Medical Section, I (1920–21), 23–29.

MAIER, MICHAEL. *De circulo physico quadrato.* Oppenheim, 1616.

———. *Symbola aureae mensae duodecim nationum.* Frankfurt a. M., 1617.

MANGET, JEAN JACQUES. See *(A) Bibliotheca chemica curiosa.*

MARIA PROPHETISSA. See *(A) Artis auriferae,* vi.

MEIER, C. A. "Moderne Physik—moderne Psychologie." In: *Die kulturelle Bedeutung der komplexen Psychologie.* Berlin, 1935. (Pp. 349–62.)

MEIER, C. A. "Spontanmanifestationen des kollektiven Unbewussten," *Zentralblatt für Psychotherapie* (Leipzig), XI (1939), 284–303.

MELCHIOR, NICHOLAS, OF HERMANNSTADT (Cibinensis) (Nicolaus Melchior Szebeni). See *(A) Theatrum chemicum,* xi.

MENNENS, GULIELMUS. See *(A) Theatrum chemicum,* xv.

MERLINUS. See *(A) Artis auriferae,* x.

MIGNE, JACQUES PAUL (ed.). *Patrologiae cursus completus.*
[*P.L.*] Latin Series. Paris, 1844–80. 221 vols.
[*P.L.*] Greek Series. Paris, 1857–66. 166 vols.
[These works are referred to as "MIGNE, *P.L.*," and "MIGNE, *P.G.*,"
respectively. References are to columns, not to pages.]

MORIENUS ROMANUS. See *(A) Artis auriferae,* xiii.

MURRAY, HENRY ALEXANDER (ed.). *Explorations in Personality.* New York and London, 1938.

"Mutus liber." See ALTUS.

MYLIUS, JOHANN DANIEL. *Philosophia reformata.* Frankfurt a. M., 1622.

NAUMANN, HANS AND IDA (trans.). *Isländische Volksmärchen.* (Die Märchen der Weltliteratur.) Jena, 1923.

NICHOLAS [KHRYPFFS] OF CUSA (Nicolaus Cusanus). *De conjecturis novissimorum temporum.* In: *Opera.* Basel, 1565.

———. *De docta ignorantia.* Edited by Paolo Rotta. Bari, 1923. For translation, see: *Of Learned Ignorance.* Translated by Germain Heron. London, 1954.

———. See also KOCH, JOSEF.

NICOLAI, CHRISTOPH FRIEDRICH. *Versuch über die Beschuldigungen, welche dem Tempelherrenorden gemacht wurden.* Berlin and Stettin, 1782.

NORTON, THOMAS. *The Ordinall of Alchimy.* With an introduction by E. J. Holmyard. London, 1928; Baltimore, 1929.

———. See also *(A) Theatrum chemicum Britannicum,* i.

NOTKER BALBULUS. *Hymnus in die Pentecostes.* See MIGNE, *P.L.*, vol. 131, cols. 1012–13.

ONIANS, RICHARD BROXTON. *The Origins of European Thought.* 2nd edn., Cambridge, 1954.

ORIGEN. *Homiliae in Leviticum*. See MIGNE, *P.G.*, vol. 12, cols. 405–574.

————. *Homiliae in librum Regnorum*. See MIGNE, *P.G.*, vol. 12, cols. 995–1028.

PARACELSUS (Theophrastus Bombast of Hohenheim). "De ente Dei." In: *Sämtliche Werke*, I. Abt.: *Medizinische . . . Schriften*, ed. K. Sudhoff and W. Matthiessen, Munich and Berlin, 1922–33, 14 vols. (Vol. I, pp. 225–233.)

————. [*Labyrinthus medicorum errantium*.] "Vom Irrgang der Arzte." In: *Sämtliche Werke* (see previous entry), vol. XI, pp. 161–221.

PAULINUS OF AQUILEIA. *Liber exhortationis ad Henricum Forojuliensem*. See MIGNE, *P.L.*, vol. 99, cols. 197–282.

PENOTUS, BERNARDUS GEORGIUS (Bernardus à Portu). See *(A) Theatrum chemicum*, **viii**.

PESTALOZZI, JOHANN HEINRICH. *Ideen*. (*Pestalozzis Werk*, edited by Martin Hürlimann, II.) Zurich, 1927.

PHILALETHES. See *(A) Musaeum hermeticum*, **iv–v**.

PLATO. *Timaeus*. For translation, see: *The Timaeus and the Critias or Atlanticus*. Translated by Thomas Taylor. (Bollingen Series III.) New York, 1944.

PLATO, pseud. See *(A) Theatrum chemicum*, **xiv**.

PORDAGE, JOHN. "Philosophisches Send-Schreiben vom Stein der Weissheit." See ROTH-SCHOLTZ.

————. *Sophia: das ist die holdseelige ewige Jungfrau der göttlichen Weisheit. . . .* Amsterdam, 1699.

PREISENDANZ, KARL (ed.). *Papyri Graecae magicae: die griechischen Zauberpapyri*. Leipzig and Berlin, 1928–31. 2 vols.

PROCLUS DIADOCHUS. *In Platonis Timaeum Commentaria*. Edited by Ernst Diehl. Leipzig, 1903–6. 3 vols. For translation, see: *The Commentaries of Proclus on the Timaeus of Plato*. Translated by Thomas Taylor. London, 1820.

RABANUS MAURUS. *Allegoriae in universam sacram Scripturam*. See MIGNE, *P.L.*, vol. 112, cols. 849–1088.

RAHNER, HUGO. "Mysterium lunae," *Zeitschrift für katholische Theologie* (Würzburg), LXIII (1939), 311–49, 428–42; LXIV (1940), 61–80, 121–31.

RASMUSSEN, KNUD. *Die Gabe des Adlers.* Frankfurt a. M., 1937.

REINACH, SALOMON. *Cultes, Mythes, et Religions.* Paris. 1905–23. 5 vols.

REITZENSTEIN, RICHARD, and SCHAEDER, HANS HEINRICH. *Studien zum antiken Synkretismus aus Iran und Griechenland.* (Studien der Bibliothek Warburg, VII.) Leipzig, 1926.

RHINE, J. B. *Extra-Sensory Perception.* Boston, 1934.

RIPLEY, GEORGE. *Omnia opera chemica.* Kassel, 1649.

Rosarium philosophorum. Secunda pars alchimiae de lapide philosophico vero modo praeparando . . . cum figuris rei perfectionem ostendentibus. Frankfurt a. M., 1550. See also *(A) Artis auriferae,* xiv.

ROSENCREUTZ, CHRISTIAN (Johann Valentin Andreae). *Chymische Hochzeit . . . anno 1459.* Reprinted from a Strasbourg 1616 edition. Edited by Ferdinand Maack. Berlin, 1913. For translation, see: *The Hermetick Romance; or, The Chymical Wedding.* Translated by E. Foxcroft. London, 1690.

———. *Turbo, sive Moleste et frustra per cuncta divagans ingenium.* Helicon, 1616.

"Rosinus ad Sarratantam." See *(A) Artis auriferae,* v.

ROTH-SCHOLTZ, FRIEDRICH (ed.). *Deutsches Theatrum chemicum.* Nuremberg, 1728–32. 3 vols. ("Philosophisches Send-Schreiben vom Stein der Weissheit," by John Pordage, vol. I, pp. 557–97).

RUSKA, JULIUS FERDINAND. *Tabula smaragdina; ein Beitrag zur Geschichte der hermetischen Literatur.* Heidelberg, 1926.

———. *Turba Philosophorum: ein Beitrag zur Geschichte der Alchemie.* (Quellen und Studien der Geschichte der Naturwissenschaften und der Medizin, I.) Berlin, 1931.

SCHENKENBACH. "Reiterlied." See his "Reuterlied" (ca. 1520), in: Franz M. Böhme (ed.). *Altdeutsches Liederbuch.* Leipzig, 1877.

[SENIOR.] *De chemia Senioris antiquissimi philosophi libellus.* Strasbourg, 1566.

SILBERER, HERBERT. *Problems of Mysticism and Its Symbolism.* Translated by Smith Ely Jelliffe. New York, 1917.

SPENCER, SIR BALDWIN, and GILLEN, FRANCIS JAMES. *The Northern Tribes of Central Australia.* London and New York, 1904.

STAPLETON, HENRY ERNEST, and HUSAIN, M. HIDAYAT (eds.). *Three Arabic Treatises on Alchemy, by Muhammad bin Umail.* (Asiatic Society of Bengal: Memoirs, XII, i.) Calcutta, 1933.

STÖCKLI, ALBAN. *Die Visionen des seligen Bruder Klaus.* Einsiedeln, 1933.

STOLCIUS DE STOLCENBERG, DANIEL. *Viridarium chymicum.* Frankfurt a. M., 1624.

"Tabula smaragdina" ("The Emerald Table of Hermes Trismegistus"). See RUSKA.

"Tractatus aureus." See *(A) Ars chemica,* i; *(A) Bibliotheca chemica curiosa,* i; *(A) Musaeum hermeticum,* i.

"Turba philosophorum." See RUSKA.

UMAIL, MUHAMMAD BIN. See STAPLETON and HUSAIN.

VANSTEENBERGHE, EDMOND. *Le Cardinal Nicolas de Cues.* Paris, 1920.

VENTURA, LAURENTIUS. See *(A) Theatrum chemicum,* x.

"Visio Arislei." See *(A) Artis auriferae,* i.

WAITE, ARTHUR EDWARD. *The Real History of the Rosicrucians.* London, 1887.

———. *The Secret Tradition in Alchemy: Its Development and Records.* London, 1926.

———. (trans.). *The Hermetic Museum Restored and Enlarged.* London, 1893. 2 vols. [A translation of *(A) Musaeum hermeticum.*]

[WEI PO-YANG.] "An Ancient Chinese Treatise on Alchemy Entitled Ts'an T'ung Ch'i, written by Wei Po-yang about 142 A.D.," translated by Lu-ch'iang Wu, *Isis* (Bruges), XVIII:53 (Oct., 1932), 210–89.

WINTHUIS, JOSEF. *Das Zweigeschlechterwesen.* Leipzig, 1928.

WOODROFFE, SIR JOHN. See AVALON.

ZACHARIUS, DIONYSUS. See *(A) Theatrum chemicum,* vi.

INDEX

INDEX

A

abaissement du niveau mental, 9; *see also* soul, loss of

Abū'l-Qāsim, 44*n*, 126

acetum fontis, see fountain, Mercurial

Acta Joannis, 36*n*

Adam, 86*n*, 96*n;* and animus, 140; sin of, 102*n;* struck by arrow, 140

adept, 57*f*, 59, 65, 98, 160*n; see also* alchemist; artifex

Adler, Alfred, 9; and incest, 15; *see also* power

Adonai, 125*n*

Adonis, 98

Aegidius de Vadis, 146*n*

"Aenigma Merlini," 102

aestheticism, 117*f*

affects, autoerotic, 106

affinity, 3, 76, 77

afflictio animae, see madness

Agrippa von Nettesheim, Cornelius, 53 and *n*

albedo, 111, 119

Albertus Magnus, 154*n*

alchemist(s): contradictions of, 125; as doctors and dream analysts, 36; as empiricists of psyche, 128*n;* — of union of opposites, 158; female, 134; and images, 126; immaturity, mental, 127, 155; obscurity of, 126*n;* pairs of, 134, 160*n;* work-room of, 35; *see also* adept; artifex

alchemy, 3*ff*, 34, *et passim;* Arabic, 83*n;* Chinese, 55; and ecclesiastical symbolism, 101; feminine element in, 134*f*, 140; *theoria* of, 159

Alfidius/Alphidius, 86, 114

Alkia, 111*n*

alter ego, 62

ambivalence, *see* Mercurius

Ambrose, St., 153*n*

analogy(-ies), 4

analysis, training, 13

analyst, *see* doctor

Anastasius Sinaita, 153*n*

Andreae, Johann Valentin, 47*n*, 54, 126*n*, 129*f*

androgyne, 149; see also *hermaphroditus*/hermaphrodite

angel, 160*n;* soul as, 139

Angelus Silesius, 110*n*, 133*n*

anima, 10, 45, 58, 59, 68, 98*f*, 140, 149; and animus, *see below;* autoerotic being, 133; as autonomous/projected part of personality, 58, 66, 83*n*, 133; *Christi,* 146; collective character, 133; effect on man's understanding, 141; ego *vs.,* 64; function of conscious/unconscious relationship, 133; as hermaphrodite, 82, 149, 157; magical aspect, 63; marriage with, 63; matrix of divine figures, 133; *anima media natura,* 82; *anima mundi, see* world-soul; as nixie, 160*n;* and numen of goddess, 67; reconciles and unites, 142; unconscious personified as, 103; "within," 67

anima and animus, 99*f;* expressed as dogma, 69; and marriage quaternity, 65; in transference, 59; unconscious personified as, 141

animal(s), *see* birds; cock/hen; crow; dog/bitch; dove; horse/donkey; lion; peacock; pelican; raven; serpent/snake

animus, 63, 68; *see also* anima and animus; discriminative function, 134, 142; illusions produced by,

The Collected Works of C. G. Jung

THE PUBLICATION of the first complete edition, in English, of the works
f C. G. Jung was undertaken by Routledge and Kegan Paul, Ltd., in
England and by Bollingen Foundation in the United States. The Ameri-
an edition is number XX in Bollingen Series, which since 1967 has been
ublished by Princeton University Press. The edition contains revised
ersions of works previously published, such as *Psychology of the Uncon-
cious*, which is now entitled *Symbols of Transformation*; works originally
written in English, such as *Psychology and Religion*; works not previously
ranslated, such as *Aion*; and, in general, new translations of virtually all
f Professor Jung's writings. Prior to his death, in 1961, the author super-
ised the textual revision, which in some cases is extensive. Sir Herbert
ead (d. 1968), Dr. Michael Fordham, and Dr. Gerhard Adler compose
ne Editorial Committee; the translator is R. F. C. Hull (except for Volume
and William McGuire is executive editor.

The price of the volumes varies according to size; they are sold sepa-
tely, and may also be obtained on standing order. Several of the volumes
e extensively illustrated. Each volume contains an index and, in most
ses, a bibliography; the final volume will contain a complete bibliography
Professor Jung's writings and a general index to the entire edition.

In the following list, dates of original publication are given in paren-
eses (of original composition, in brackets). Multiple dates indicate
visions.

* Published 1961.
† Published 1956; 2nd edn., 1967. (65 plates, 43 text figures.)

* Published 1953; 2nd edn., 1966.
† Published 1960; 2nd edn., 1969.

* Published 1959; 2nd edn., 1968. (Part I: 79 plates, with 29 in colour.)

* Published 1964; 2nd edn., 1970. (8 plates.)
† Published 1958; 2nd edn., 1969.

* Published 1953; 2nd edn., completely revised, 1968. (270 illustrations.)
† Published 1968. (50 plates, 4 text figures.)
‡ Published 1963; 2nd edn., 1970. (10 plates.)

* Published 1966.
† Published 1954; 2nd edn., revised and augmented, 1966. (13 illustrations.)
‡ Published 1954.